FAVELIZATION: THE IMAGINARY BRAZIL IN CONTEMPORARY FILM, FASHION, AND DESIGN

Favelization:

The Imaginary Brazil in Contemporary Film, Fashion, and Design

By Adriana Kertzer

New York, NY

To B.R.G.

CONTENTS

INTRODUCTION

I am drawn to issues of design and national identity because of an enduring sense of displacement. I grew up in São Paulo between 1979 and 1997, the daughter of a Texan mother and first-generation Brazilian father, himself the son of a Bessarabian father and Cuban-born grandmother whose family was from Odessa. Like many of my peers at Escola Graduada (the American school), I grew up bilingual and feeling out of place both in Brazil and the United States. While people in my hometown often told me I was "not really Brazilian," once I moved to the United States in 1998, I had to get used to the words "exotic" and "Brasileira" pronounced with a thick pseudo-Latin accent. I continue to live today in a state of national suspension.

To say that I am fixated on issues of national identity is an understatement. It is no surprise that this interest became an obsession in my career as a design academic as well. My sense of hybridity makes me particularly sensitive to nationalistic language: I understand the difficulty in defining Brazilianness on a personal level and, as a result, approach generalizations about what "Brazilian" is with skepticism. I also have a preference for definitions that allow for ambiguity and openness. The research presented in this book reflects my discomfort with a contemporary trend I refer to as favelization: the use of references to Brazilian favelas to market luxury products to a primarily non-Brazilian audience.[1] I am not speaking of the general fascination with favelas among social scientists and development workers; it is explicitly commercial endeavors that continue to interest me.

Favelas are the informal squatter settlements that grow along the hillsides and lowlands of many Brazilian cities.[2] Most favelados (the inhabitants of favelas) are immigrants from the northeast of Brazil, indigenous people or descendants of slaves. Not all urban poor live in favelas, nor are all favelados poor.[3] However, one can generalize that most favelados are socioeconomically disadvantaged. Yet despite the negative connotations attached to favelas by Brazilian media and public policy, and the fact that most middle- and upper-class Brazilians shun these spaces, apparel companies, furniture designers, artists, restaurateurs, and filmmakers use references to favelas to brand their products, projects, or spaces as "Brazilian." As mentioned earlier, their target audience is almost always non-Brazilian. Often, the luxury objects in question bear little or no resemblance to favelas themselves or to what favelados can afford.[4]

The three case studies discussed here explore different

---

1. Frederico Duarte, "O Fator Favela," *Projeto Design* 376 (June 2011); Perlman, 1075-86. Other authors, such as Frederico Duarte and Janice Perlman, identify this phenomenon using different terminology such as "favela factor" and "favela chic." The word "favelization" has also been used in other contexts to describe, for example, the increased number of favelas in a given region of the world. It was also used by the music group Afroreggae as the name for one of its international tours.

2. Marcio Fortes de Almeida, Ministério das Cidades–Plano Nacional de Habitação (Brasília, Distrito Federal: Secretaria Nacional de Habitação, 2010), 37.

3. Davis, 530-34.

4. The term "luxury" here is defined as nonessential consumption.

Multi-story buildings in favela Rocinha photographed during a visit with the company Favela Tour on December 30, 2011. Photograph by the author.

aspects of favelization in film, fashion, and furniture; I hope my research furthers the debate about how design reflects and exacerbates complex power relations. What intrigues me about references to favelas in the context of luxury goods is that few of the people making these statements are from favelas. I am fascinated by the disconnect between how I experienced (or not) favelas growing up as a privileged Brazilian, and the frequency with which it is referenced in the marketing of design projects aimed at a foreign audience. Even though I grew up in São Paulo, and favelas are a fact of life in Brazilian urban centers, the first time I entered a favela was to conduct research for this project. These communities were a "part" of my life in the same way they are for many of the producers discussed here. From the dining room window of the apartment I lived in, I could see

Paraisópolis, one of the largest favelas in São Paulo. But my daily activities did not bring me within its premises, and many people who provided essential services to my family lived in them but were not a part of our social circle. I therefore recognize the limits of my awareness of favelas. In fact, I refuse to speak with any authority about the realities of these communities. What I do choose to speak forcefully about is the circulation of stereotypes in the context of the international luxury market.

PRIMITIVISM, EXOTICISM, AND THE IMPACT OF DESIGN

How have favelas become signifiers of Brazilianness and why are they used to market luxury products? The country has long been stereotyped as tropical, fun, musical, beautiful, and lawless; its inhabitants sexual, gregarious, flexible, great at soccer, and dark(er)-skinned. Producers of contemporary Brazilian culture have added favelas to the list. In fact, references to favelas have become increasingly common (and popular) since the early 1990s as hallmarks of contemporary Brazilianness because of their interaction with established stereotypes about Brazil. The goal of this book is to further a discussion of how Brazilians and non-Brazilians employ certain spaces, people, and social issues to imbue design projects with a sense of the exotic. Favelization is a process through which something that has been maligned throughout Brazilian history is transformed into a signifier of attached value, stereotypes, "coolness," and Brazilianness.

Design and marketing have often been the mediums through which these fantasies are given form and fuel. In *Gone Primitive: Savage Intellects, Modern Lives,* Mariana Torgovnick discusses the intersection between commodification, marketing, and tropes of primitivism:

> In the deflationary era of postmodernism, the primitive often frankly loses any particular identity and even its sense of being "out there"; it merges into a generalized, marketable thing–a grab-bag primitive in which urban and rural, modern and traditional Africa and South American and Asia and the Middle-East merge into a common locale called the third world which exports garments and accessories, music, ideologies, and styles for Western, and especially urban Western, consumption.[5]

Certain things deemed primitive (such as favelas and favelados) are commodified by becoming "marketable things." Torgovnick's analysis is particularly helpful to an understanding of favelization because it shows how a highly edited and stylized treatment of favelas connects with consumption. The case studies I discuss involve exaggerated generalizations about Brazilian favelas. For example, press releases, blog posts, and websites use the words "Brazilian favelas" as if it were unimportant which favela might have inspired an actual design. Yet these terms are used because "the favela" has become a "grab-bag primitive" that increases a design's attached value and a luxury item's emotional appeal.

Contemporary fascination with favelas is the result of multiple factors. It is partly due to increased attention among social scientists, who have turned favelas into the world's most studied low-income communities.[6] Academics often act as intermediaries between favelas and formal Brazilian cities, institutions of political power, and cultural capital.[7] In doing so, they increase national and international awareness of these communities.

5. Mariana Torgovnick, *Gone Primitive: Savage Intellects, Modern Lives* (Chicago: University of Chicago Press, 1991), 37.

6. Janice Perlman, *Favela: Four Decades of Living on the Edge in Rio de Janeiro* (New York: Oxford University Press, 2011). Kindle edition. Highlight Loc. 1075-86.

However, while academics may be partly responsible for the growing visibility of favelas, I argue that certain types of material culture have become the main intermediaries between favela and non-favela inhabitants. Social scientists may play an important role in describing the reality of favelas, but film, marketing campaigns, and consumer products have fueled the international fascination with favelas we witness today.

Changes in attitudes about subcultures, and about Brazil's favelas specifically, have also spurred favelization. The rise of rap culture and "ghetto fabulous" style during the 1980s and 1990s might be seen as a precursor to favelization. Both trends took the population and social issues of certain urban spaces and turned them into fetishized commodified styles. Ghetto fabulous (and later favelization) also became increasingly popular through the increased visual representation of these urban spaces in film. Music videos and movies disseminated a large volume of images of ghetto fashion, fashion, and lifestyle.[8] Similarly, Brazilians and non-Brazilians have gained "access" to favelas through music videos, documentaries, fictional films, and even favela tours.[9] This visual access

7. Licia do Prado Valladares, *A invenção da favela: do mito de origem à favela* (Rio de Janeiro: Editora FGV, 2005).

8. Lyneise E. Williams, "Heavy Metal: Decoding Hip-Hop Jewelry," *Metalsmith* 27, no. 1 (2007): 26–41. Williams discusses how jewelry in hip-hop culture "is elevated from benign accessories to symbols of economic power."

9. Barbara Kirshenblatt-Gimblett, *Destination Culture: Tourism, Museums, and Heritage* (Berkeley: University of California Press, 1998), 54. Most favela tours are currently offered in Rio de Janeiro and focus on Rocinha (with Vila das Canoas as a shorter stop). I went on two different tours, one run by the company Favela Tours and the other by an individual who refers to himself as Zezinho da Rocinha. Kirshenblatt-Gimblett contextualizes the favela tour within the history of ethnographic displays and tourism. She notes: "Historically, ethnography has constituted its subjects at the margins of geography, history, and society. Not surprisingly, then, in a convergence

both demystified and re-mystified favelas, turning something that is not exotic into something titillating, mysterious, and even mythical. Trends like ghetto fabulous and favelization require a careful consideration of how poverty, disadvantage, and discrimination become reconfigured as commercialized signifiers.

Just because favelas are mentioned in regard to certain luxury goods does not mean these communities are being "seen." Invisibility leads people to believe details are unnecessary; it allows for the treatment of all favelas and their realities as interchangeable, whereas specificity is a sign of attention, respect, and deeper understanding–especially given the heterogeneity among favelas and within them. The concept of marginality may have been debunked, deconstructed, dismissed, rediscovered, and reconstructed by academics and politicians.[10] But seeing these in terms of design and marketing is another thing: favelization is one example of how artists, designers, filmmakers, and entrepreneurs reconstruct interpretations of marginalized peoples and spaces for purposes of commercialization. Otherness remains a sales tool. The issues of (in)visibility and commercialized marginality are therefore tied to larger

of moral adventure, social exploration, and sensation seeking, the inner city is constructed as a socially distant but physically proximate exotic–and erotic–territory. Visits to this territory tempt the adventurer to cross the dangerous line between voyeurism and acting out. Slumming, like tourism more generally, takes the spectator to the site, and as areas are canonized in a geography of attractions, whole territories become extended ethnographic theme parks. An ethnographic bell jar drops over the terrain. A neighborhood, village, or region becomes for all intents and purposes a living museum in situ. The museum effect, rendering the quotidian spectacular, becomes ubiquitous."

10. Perlman, 2818-21.

A tourist (left) has his picture taken with Zezinho da Rocinha (owner of Favela Adventures) during a favela tour in Rocinha on January 2, 2012. Photograph by the author.

questions of power, domination, co-optation, and exploitation.

A discussion of favelization is bound to be complex, controversial, and uncomfortable. Can favelization increase the invisibility and marginalization of favelas? Does a mere reference to favelas in a commercial context exacerbate the political, economic, and social asymmetry prevalent in Brazil? If the answer to these questions is yes, then favelization may have serious material, cultural, historical, sociopsychological, and political consequences.[11] However, many believe the references to favelas in design projects are innocuous and even further awareness of certain socioeconomic issues in Brazil. They argue that favelization might lead to improvements in the lives of favelados because this trend increases their visibility internationally. I do not believe this to be the case. References and depictions of favelas are not neutral repetitions of fact–they are usually stylized and curated. This book does not focus on whether the references are correct or beneficial, but on the social and economic system in which they are embedded.[12] In fact, the most interesting designs have political consequences that transcend the simple categories of accurate and inaccurate, intended and unintended.[13] Understanding favelization may involve discussions about designers' intentions, but my focus is on how it has become a trend that may exacerbate unequal power relations. My objective is not to settle any of the issues presented here once and for all, but to indicate general dimensions and significance.[14]

How did a symbol of Brazil's poverty, much maligned by the Brazilian press and often feared by inhabitants of the formal city, come to signify Brazilianness and attached value? Is favelization evidence of a deeper cultural shift in which Brazil's poverty is repositioned as part of its national brand? Or is something else at stake in these endeavors that makes favelization a patronizing and opportunistic way of portraying the reality of a certain segment of the Brazilian population, fetishizing a space and its inhabitants, to brand products as Brazilian? These questions require that we address the difference between

---

11. Ibid., 2896-2909.
12. Langdon Winner, "Do Artifacts Have Politics?" *Daedalus* 109, no. 1 (Winter, 1980), 122.
13. Ibid., 125.
14. Ibid., 123.

the meanings attached to favelas in Brazil and those employed by companies and individuals using references to favelas in the marketing of high-end products. They also challenge the myths of racial democracy and intersocial class cordiality common in mainstream discourse about Brazil. It becomes impossible to talk about the role of favelas in Brazilian society without addressing discrimination based on race, socioeconomic background, and place of residence. At the same time, favelization highlights a persistent need for the exotic among consumers. While I acknowledge that each project, artist, designer, and filmmaker has its/his/her own set of objectives and biases, I hope this book calls attention to trends in which we, as consumers, may be complicit.

METHODOLOGY AND OVERVIEW OF CHAPTERS

I wrote each chapter of this book as a paper for a different course of the masters program in the History of the Decorative Arts and Design co-sponsored by Parsons The New School for Design and the Cooper-Hewitt, National Design Museum. My thesis was the first in the history of the masters program to deal with contemporary design from Latin America; this book is also the Cooper-Hewitt's first publication dedicated primarily to Latin American design. My hope is that this book stimulates transnational debate about design, national identity, and ethics–and represents one small step towards making design history more inclusive. I believe that favelization will emerge as one of the most important aspects of postmodern Brazilian design and identity because at the center of this debate are issues of ethics, the potential impact of cultural production, and questions about the appropriate responses to the use of references to underprivileged communities in a commercial setting. As design academics and school curricula draw attention to the design histories of regions of the world until now regarded as peripheral, I believe trends such as favelization will become a leading focal point. Favelization.net offers additional examples of favelization and allows for the continued exploration of this trend beyond the publication date of this book.

Other terms have been used to describe favelization such as "favela chic," "favela factor," and "slumification." I chose the word favelization because the suffix "-tion" highlights its existence as a process, one that entails some form of transformation and manipulation. I was influenced and inspired by the writings of design critic Frederico Duarte and his website Alvorada.org. Yet while authors before me have questioned designers' use of references to favelas, their writing focuses on listing examples and identifying potential issues (rather than investigating them in depth and contextualizing favelization within a larger theoretical framework). I drew on publications by scholars in cultural and postcolonial studies including John Tagg, Zygmunt Bauman, Edward Said, Mariana Torgovnick, Mike Davis, and Trinh T. Minh-Ha. Lastly, while written material about favelization in film, fashion, and design exists, this book creates a bridge between these previously disparate discussions.

A case study approach was used to allow for an in-depth discussion of the written and visual materials related to a specific project, as well as a lengthy theoretical analysis. However, there are certain drawbacks associated with the use of case studies, such as the potential perception that the examples chosen are the only ones (or the most significant). They are not.

The subjects of my writing are divided into three general categories: producers, consumers, and residents of favelas. I believe, with near certainty, that there is very limited overlap (if any) between these categories. In fact, this lack of overlap is a characteristic of favelization. When I criticize certain individuals for "using" Brazil, I do so with humility. I have done the same. To promote my own projects at different points in my career, I drew on the numerous stereotypes associated with the country. My livelihood (like that of many of the producers mentioned here) has often depended on capitalizing on knowledge of Brazilian culture, language, and relationships. Yet as a lawyer at a large corporate law firm in New York working primarily on Brazilian capital market transactions, I became aware of how selective Brazilian national identity could be in a transnational, commercial setting. My primary responsibility was helping Brazilian corporations explain their products and value to non-Brazilian investors. This experience made me sensitive to the importance of branding and the process of selling a story, product, or investment. It also influences how I think about ethics, power relations, the structure of economic relationships, and the complex economics of cultural projects today.

I refrained from describing certain individuals, companies, and projects according to their nationality when I deemed such descriptions problematic. It is often impossible to identify a project solely through a reference to the nationality of its figurehead. Furthermore, just because someone is Brazilian does not mean they have been to a favela (much less lived in one). A discussion of favelization requires the inclusion of Brazilians, non-Brazilian natives, and individuals whose life experiences challenge traditional notions of nationality. Favelization requires one to think carefully about what is "Brazilian," who is "foreign" and who is "Brazilian." It is a powerful example of how cultural trends are the result of active exchanges between nations as well as unequal power dynamics within a nation. My perspective therefore is supra-national, anti-territorial, and anti-national, because favelization challenges conventional territorial demarcations and traditional understandings of national identities.

One question that remains unanswered is: Does favelization benefit favelas? I believe it is impossible to say. What methods would we use to measure impact? How do we draw a connection between the case studies set forth here and favelas? The difficulty of measuring the impact of favelization–both positive and negative–is perhaps what makes it such an interesting issue. It is also beyond the scope of my research. While I allow for the possibility that favelization may entail some positive impact, this book does not attempt to measure it.

To address the larger issues related to favelization, I dedicate the rest of this introduction to a discussion of Brazilian identity, the history of favelas, public policies towards favelas in Brazil, and the place favelas have within mainstream Brazilian culture. In the next chapter, "Favelization in Film," I discuss favelization in the context of music videos, movies, and documentaries because these types of cultural production have been most effective in molding, changing, or reinforcing perceptions of favelas in Brazil and abroad. My case study analysis focuses on the fictional film *City of God* (2002) and the documentary *Waste Land* (2010). The overwhelming number of movies released since 1996 about Rio de Janeiro's slums or the city's history of crime, combined with their far-reaching international dissemination, means that images of favelas have reached a large number of people, most of whom have never entered one. I believe that the marketing of luxury items using references to favelas would not be possible were it not for the existence and dissemination of these films. Furthermore, film provide a context for the exploration of four themes recurrent in favelization: interpretation, transcendence, aestheticization, and domination. Favelization in film often involves the interplay of these themes, as well as the repetition of familiar tropes related to the Primitive, Otherness, and manufactured exoticism.

The chapter "Favelization in Fashion" focuses on the 2009 Campanas + Lacoste project, a collaboration between the French clothing brand Lacoste and the designers Humberto and Fernando Campana (the Campanas). In 2006, Lacoste launched a Holiday Collector's Series, which is a yearly collaboration with designers to create a limited edition of polo shirts. The Campanas + Lacoste 2009 project resulted in six types of shirts, the most expensive of which sold for US$7,000. This case study focuses on the references to favelas in the Campanas + Lacoste marketing materials. The Campanas are Brazil's most famous contemporary designers and their work often references Brazilian themes. Brazilianness is an important aspect of the Campanas' production and the marketing of their luxury products outside Brazil. In my discussion of the advertising and press coverage of the shirts designed by the Campanas for Lacoste, I explore how an international clothing company and the Campanas use references to favelas to brand a line of luxury products as Brazilian. This chapter discusses theories of commodification, fetishization, and the use/creation of a primitive Other in the process of defining national identity. It also brings up important issues about power relations among unequal economic actors.

"Favelization in Design" focuses on Brunno Jahara's Neorustica high-end furniture line in which each object is named after a favela in Rio de Janeiro and Design da Gema's Stray Bullet chair and Pacification shelves designed by David Elia. While there are significant differences between Jahara and Elia, they are both Brazilian designers in their thirties who employ the tropes associated with favelas to brand high-end furniture as "Brazilian." Jahara and Elia returned to Brazil in 2009 and 2010, respectively, after spending several years studying and working abroad. In my analysis, I argue that Jahara and Elia are replicating a tactic used successfully by their predecessors: blending strategic references to Brazil's poverty with fantasy and desire in the service of commerce. This chapter first explores the objects themselves and the language the designers use to increase the appeal of their furniture among non-Brazilian consumers. I then situate the objects within a larger discussion about exoticism, primitivism, the carnivalesque, and domestication.

BRAZILIAN IDENTITY

Brazilian identity is constantly being redefined. This statement is successfully argued by Jeffrey Lesser in *Negotiating National Identity*, a book about how immigration in the twentieth century challenged Brazil's imagined uniform identity. Lesser argues that there is no static or monolithic definition of Brazilian identity and that "the apparently static elite discourse was in fact ambiguous."[15] I agree with Lesser's contention that "Brazil remains a country where hyphenated ethnicity is predominant yet unacknowledged."[16] Yet while Lesser would say the source of the hyphen is primarily ethnicity, I would argue it can also be social class and the benefits wealth can provide (such as educational and work opportunities outside Brazil). A rich Brazilian is different from a favelado-Brazilian in numerous and significant ways.

In discussing favelization, I challenge common tropes of contemporary Brazilianness, such as the notion that favelas represent an essential Brazilian trait: improvisation in the face of need. Such traits are not necessarily the exclusive domain of Brazilians; they are shared by poor populations around the world. In challenging such stereotypes I hope to further a deeper analysis of how Brazilian poverty is being portrayed by individuals who are often middle- and upper-class, regardless of their nationality.[17] I question how favelas are represented in the work of contemporary filmmakers and designers, all the while acknowledging that they are being refiltered through my own selection and analysis.

Furthermore, how Brazilians define national identity is often influenced by how Brazil is perceived by foreigners. The 2012 contemporary art and design exhibit *From the Margin to the Edge: Brazilian Art and Design in the 21st Century* questioned the clichés related to Brazil. In fact, one section was dedicated to challenging the dichotomy between notions of "savage" and "civilized." The curator, Rafael Cardoso, discussed the influence of

15. Jeffrey Lesser, *Negotiating National Identity* (Durham, NC: Duke University Press, 1999), 2.

16. Ibid.

17. Frederico Duarte, "Beyond the Fruit Hat: Brazilian Product and Furniture Design Today," referencing Maria Tommasini and Francesca Picchi, "Design Morbido/Soft Design," *Domus* 848 (May 2002). See also Vik Muniz, "Campana Brothers," *Bomb* 102 (Winter 2008), 2.

foreigners' perceptions of Brazilianness in an online video about the exhibit:

> The way Europeans view Brazil is still frequently anthropological [and] ethnographic. And the way Brazilians see themselves is often through this ethnographic European gaze. Brazilians think of themselves according to notions such as "savage", according to notions of "civilized" and "not civilized." ... What you think about Brazil, even if you are Brazilian, is perhaps not as simple as we tend to imagine.[18]

Cardoso stresses the permeability of Brazilian national identity and the influence of the foreign gaze. While he references only Europeans in his analyses, American perceptions of Brazil are an equally important influence on Brazilian self-perception. The permeability of identity means that when a particular aspect of Brazilian society not commonly deemed "desirable" becomes popular outside of Brazil, this external attention often results in a reframing of attitudes within the country. Such is the case with favelas.

Favelization is a hybrid multinational process. In 1928, Oswald de Andrade published the *Manifesto*

---

18. "O olhar do europeu para o Brasil ainda é frequentemente antropológico é etnográfico. E o olhar do brasileiro para si mesmo é frequentemente este olhar europeu etnográfico. O brasileiro si pensa a partir de conceitos como "selvagem"; com a idéia de o "civilizado" e "não civilizado.".... [O] que você pensa sobre o Brasil, mesmo se você for brasileiro, talvez as coisas não sejam tão simples com oagente costuma imaginar," video clip, accessed on October 15, 2012, youtube, http://youtu.be/46rzksttKJ8. Translation by the author. The exhibit was on display at the Somerset House in London between July 21, 2012, and September 8, 2012 (overlapping with the 2012 Olympic games). See the website of Somerset House. The exhibit was part of the larger project Rio Occupation London, which brought the work of thirty artists/designers from Rio de Janeiro to London during the 2012 Olympic Games. Events were hosted at the Battersea Arts Centre, Somerset House, Victoria and Albert Museum, and other venues across London. Rio Occupation London was commissioned by Rio de Janeiro's State Culture Secretariat and produced by the People's Palace Projects and Battersea Arts Centre. See the website of Rio Occupation London.

Antropôfago (a.k.a. *Manifesto Antropofágico*), in which he advocated in favor of Brazilian intellectuals' appropriating European metropolitan culture, digesting it and producing something hybrid and singular of their own.[19] As Adriano Pedrosa suggested in ArtNexusBrasilen Colombia, we are experiencing an inversion of the *Manifesto Antropôfago* eighty-four years after Andrade published it; Brazilian culture itself is being appropriated by non-Brazilians who reference its art, architecture, music, and poetry.[20] I add to Pedrosa's list favelas. Today, both Brazilian and foreign designers, marketing professionals, and filmmakers interpret and appropriate favelas, often producing something hybrid, something that merely touches on reality but does not reproduce it.[21] More importantly, the inversion of *antropôfagia* means that Brazilian identity itself is being created through a hybrid process, one in which individuals of varied national backgrounds influence what can be considered "Brazilian."

19. Adriano Pedrosa, ed., *ArtNexusBrasil en Colombia* (Bogota, Colombia: Arte en Colombia SAS, 2011), 9.
20. Ibid.
21. Cristovão Duarte, "A reinvenção da cidade a partir dos espaços populares" (paper presented at the O que é a favela, afinal? conference, Maré, Rio de Janeiro, August 19-20, 2009). Duarte noted: "An extensive production of documentaries, films, photographs, songs, books, academic theses, produced, in the majority of cases, by the inhabitants of the favelas, as well as numerous cultural projects connected to the Hip-Hop movement, surface in the national and international scene, including from the urbanistic point of view, as places where identities are lived and produced, [identities] that refuse the condition of ghetto or spaces of segregation within a divided city." Duarte argues that "in the majority of cases" this cultural production is generated by favelados. Whether this is the case or not lies beyond the scope of book. However, the examples I have chosen challenge this assertion.

DEFINING FAVELAS

In its 2012 census, the Instituto Brasileiro de Geografia e Estatística defined favelas as "subnormal agglomerate[s,] any settlement with a minimum of 51 household units, mostly in need of essential public services, occupying or having occupied until recently a third-party property–public or private–and generally arranged in a disordered and dense way."[22] The likely source of the Brazilian name for these settlements is the favela bush, a plant that grows in the caatingas of northeastern Brazil and is eaten by animals (especially during the droughts that frequently afflict the region).[23] The favela bush grew in the stony soil of the Arraial de Canudos, and the term was later used to describe the area where the soldiers who fought in the Canudos War settled in Rio de Janeiro.[24] By the 1920s, favela became the generic term for a squatter settlement in Brazil.[25]

During the first decades of the twentieth century, immigrants from the countryside built favelas on illegally occupied lands near or inside major Brazilian cities.[26] Immigrants moved to the cities in search of jobs, fleeing droughts in the northeast and the spread of industrial-scale agribusiness.[27] However, most sold all they owned to pay for their travel and arrived in the city with no

22. "2010 Census Improved Identification of Subnormal Agglomerates", IBGE, accessed [n.d.].
23. Ivan Maurício, "<a href="http://www.onordeste.com/onordeste/ enciclopediaNordeste/index.php?titulo=FavelaEnciclopédia Nordeste: Favela Urbana", O Nordeste, accessed October 12, 2012.
24. Ibid.
25. Perlman, 856-58.
26. Fernando L. Lara, "Vila Viva Favela Redesign" (lecture, Parsons New School For Design, New York, NY, November 2, 2011), handwritten notes by the author.
27. Mike Davis, Planet of Slums (London: Verso, 2007). Kindle edition. Highlight Loc. 263-66.

money for housing. These immigrants solved their housing problems in any way they could, often by building shacks on vacant lands. As a result, favelas grew in the outskirts of cities and in the immediate vicinity of the formal city, usually in unused or undesirable pieces of land such as steep hillsides, tidal marshes, flood-prone swamps, and garbage dumps.[28] The government sporadically removed favelas if the land was of interest to private owners or state agencies. Nevertheless, many of these informal dwellings endured in areas where land was deemed unworthy of development, and became larger communities with distinctive personalities.[29]

Favelas are characterized by an organic visual composition. Construction often follows the local topography instead of the orthogonal grids common in formal cities. Yet despite their similar organic curves, the physical characteristics of individual favelas differ.[30] Some favela homes are barracos, huts made primarily out of wood, sheet metal, and construction-site discards. Other dwellings are made of brick and cement, and several stories high. Many favela homes are made of columns that rest on a foundation slab, have support beams, a roof slab, and walls of exposed bricks. Almost all favela homes are designed, built, and occupied by their owners. They usually do not conform to the building codes imposed in the formal city and often lack the infrastructure and social services available in other urban areas.

The demographic profile of Brazilian favelas is complex.

28. Cristóvão Duarte, "A reinvenção da cidade a partir dos espaços populares."
   See also Perlman, 551-54 and 899-901.
29. Perlman, 186-95.
30. Perlman, 209-11.

Photograph. Partial view of the favela Catacumba on Avenida Epitácio Pessoa, Rio de Janeiro, 1968. Janice Perlman. Courtesy of Janice Perlman, author of *Favela: Four Decades of Living on the Edge in Rio de Janeiro* (Oxford University Press, 2010) and Founder & President of the Mega-Cities Project (www.megacitiesproject.org).

Favelas are heterogeneous racially, culturally, and economically–and there is also variation among favelas.[31] As noted earlier, not all urban poor live in favelas, nor are all favelados poor.[32] Favelados are linked economically and politically to the formal city, but they are exploited, manipulated, and stigmatized within Brazil's intricate and powerful class system. Yet despite these nuances, favelization reinforces the idea that Brazil's favelas are similar to each other, and that favelados are homogeneous and are somehow different from other Brazilians.

31. Perlman, 3070-72.
32. Davis, 530-34.

Photograph. View of the favela Catacumba from the Lagoa Rodrigo de Freitas in Rio de Janeiro, 1969. Janice Perlman. Courtesy of Janice Perlman, author of *Favela: Four Decades of Living on the Edge in Rio de Janeiro* (Oxford University Press, 2010) and Founder & President of the Mega-Cities Project (www.megacitiesproject.org).

It is impossible to discuss the Brazilian favelas without acknowledging the country's socioeconomic inequality. Although levels of absolute poverty in other regions of the developing world exceed those in Latin America, Brazil has the highest level of inequality. According to the World Bank, Brazil is third on the list of countries with the worst income disparity.[33] The richest twenty percent of Brazilians earn almost sixty percent of the national income, and the poorest twenty percent earn approximately two and a half percent.[34] In this respect,

33. "Income Inequality," *The Economist*, April 20, 2011.
34. Martin Matter, "Brazil's Economy: An Introduction," Swiss Business HUB Brazil (2012): 5, accessed October 12, 2012.

Photograph. View of the former site of the favela Catacumba as seen from the Lagoa Rodrigo de Freitas in 1999 (the favela was removed in 1970). Janice Perlman. Courtesy of Janice Perlman, author of *Favela: Four Decades of Living on the Edge in Rio de Janeiro* (Oxford University Press, 2010) and Founder & President of the Mega-Cities Project (www.megacitiesproject.org).

Brazil is also the most unequal among countries of its size.[35] Furthermore, while several small Third World countries (e.g., Haiti, Paraguay, Sierra Leone, Namibia, and Botswana) have greater inequality, their economies are not as large, developed, or as vibrant as Brazil's.[36] The recent economic boom may have improved the lives of lower-class Brazilians, but it has not necessarily made Brazilian society less unequal.

35. "Brazil Overview–Context", The World Bank (2012), accessed October 12, 2012, stating that Brazil is the "world's seventh wealthiest economy (2011 GDP US$2.2 trillion) and "the largest country in area and population in Latin America and the Caribbean."
36. Perlman, 1235-40.

Photograph. Rio favela in early stage of development on a flood plain, 1968. Janice Perlman. Courtesy of Janice Perlman, author of *Favela: Four Decades of Living on the Edge in Rio de Janeiro* (Oxford University Press, 2010) and Founder & President of the Mega-Cities Project (www.megacitiesproject.org).

The high degree of inequality in Brazil is evident in the landscape and streets of Brazilian cities. Favelas are one visual manifestation of income inequality in Brazil. Rio de Janeiro is perhaps the city in which the contrast between rich and poor is most obvious. Certain parts of Rio resemble a First World city, with expensive commercial establishments, high finance, high technology, high fashion, and high culture. Other parts of the city are characteristically Third World due to high infant mortality, malnutrition, unemployment, homelessness, and the presence of contagious diseases.[37] As a result, "[t]he difference between the upscale bairros of Lagoa, Leblon, Ipanema, and Jardim Botânico and the

37. Ibid., 574-77 and 1241-48.

Location where household trash is left to be picked up by sanitation trucks in favela Rocinha, photographed during a tour led by Zezinho da Rocinha on January 2, 2012. Photograph by the author.

popular bairros such as Tijuca, Irajá, and São Gonçalo show up on the Human Development Index as the same difference from Belgium and Burkina Faso."[38] This statistic is one way of interpreting the vastly different realities of Rio's population. Violence (a common theme in favelization) is one consequence of inequality in Brazil. In 2011, the United Nations Office on Drugs and Crime (UNODC) released its first "Global Study on Homicide," stating that countries with wide income disparities are four times more likely to be afflicted by violent crime than more equitable societies.[39] The levels of government

38. Ibid., 995-97.
39. "2011 Global Study on Homicide," UNODC, accessed on October 15, 2012, . The report posits that "stark inequalities and social/spatial segregation,..can foster criminal behaviours." See also "2011 Global Study on Homicide: Trends, Contexts, Data" accessed on October 15, 2012, (p. 78).

services vary greatly in Brazilian cities and in favelas. In some favelas, residents lack running water and access to electricity.[40] Some favelas receive electricity by way of illegal connections hooked into power lines. However, many favelas today have running water and their residents receive individualized electricity bills. Furthermore, sewage lines, schools, and healthcare are available in some favelas, while in others these public services are nonexistent. In short, it is impossible to generalize about favela construction and infrastructure. Yet, even though by the mid-twentieth century many favela structures were already built of brick and concrete, a stereotype that prevails is that of the wooden barraco, deprivation, and informality.[41]

It is important to note that favelization's popularity has spread at the same time poor populations around the world have faced increasingly limited access to formal housing. The history of favelas is similar to that of other squatter settlements in the Third World.[42] Squatter settlements represent an attempt by the world's poorest populations to meet their housing needs in light of national and local governments' incapacity or refusal to provide adequate housing. According to Mike Davis in *Planet of Slums,* the formal housing markets in the Third World provide approximately twenty percent of new housing stock. This lack of formal housing leads people to rely on self-built shanties, informal rentals, pirate subdivisions, or the sidewalks. Since 1970, slum growth in the Third World has outpaced urbanization, as illegal

40. Laura Machado de Mello Bueno, "Contribuição para o conhecimento sobre as favelas no Brasil" (paper presented at the O que é a favela, afinal? conference, Maré, Rio de Janeiro, August 19-20, 2009).
41. Lara, "Modernism Made Vernacular: The Brazilian Case," 46-47.
42. Perlman, 2795.

or informal land markets become the most common additions to the housing stock. Before World War II, most poor urban Latin Americans lived in inner-city rental housing. However, after World War II many Latin American cities experienced a dramatic increase in squatter settlements.[43] The glamorization of Brazil's squatter settlements becomes ever more troubling given the lack of available choice; a lack of access to housing has made favelas the only option in terms of new housing stock for many poor Brazilians.

PUBLIC POLICIES TOWARDS FAVELAS IN BRAZIL

Government policies in Brazil directed at favelas have often favored removal rather than the creation of housing alternatives. In response to the growth of shantytowns, authorities in several Latin American countries, supported by the urban middle classes, have launched massive crackdowns on informal settlements.[44] In Brazil, favelados are often deemed to be the source of many urban problems such as crime, violence, promiscuity, the breakdown of traditional family structures, and "the creation of a culture of poverty"; favelas are seen as "a transfer of poverty from the rural areas to the city" and threat to the well-being of Brazilian cities.[45] The government's refusal to provide running water and electricity to favelas has created a danger to public health.[46] Policies that have favored removal create a vicious cycle in which lack of infrastructure development

43. Davis, 268-73, 728-31, 1286-91.
44. Ibid., 1286-91.
45. "Development of Rio de Janeiro," Unlocking Archives: Royal Geographical Society with The Institute of British Geographers, accessed October 12, 2012.
46. Davis, 212-214.

leads to conditions deemed unsanitary, and criminalization of certain housing structures leads to their unregulated growth.[47] Discrimination has also been an important factor in the policies of Latin American governments. Since many of the new urban immigrants have been indigenous peoples or descendants of slaves, there has often been a racial dimension to governments' "war on squatting."[48] Favelas have been under the threat of removal since they first appeared on Brazil's urban landscape. The upcoming 2014 World Cup and 2016 Olympics have led to questions about the potential increased risk of displacement.[49] Davis notes that:

> In the urban Third World, poor people dread high-profile international events–conferences, dignitary visits, sporting events, beauty contests, and international festivals–that prompt authorities to launch crusades to clean up the city: slum-dwellers know that they are the "dirt" or "blight" that their governments prefer the world not to see….These days governments are more likely to improve the view by razing the slums and driving the residents out of the city.[50]

47. Perlman, 2896-909. Perlman notes that the dehumanization and criminalization of the poor, as well as the way they have been rendered invisible, "has been developed into a body of literature with its own set of concepts and assumptions."
48. Davis, 1286-91.
49. "ONU acusa Brasil de desalojar pessoas à força por conta da Copa e Olimpíada," O Estado de São Paulo, April 26, 2011, h. The article describes how people are being displaced in cities such as São Paulo, Rio de Janeiro, Belo Horizonte, Curitiba, Porto Alegre, Recife, Natal, and Fortaleza in a manner that could be deemed a violation of human rights.
50. Davis, 2445-58. Davis states, "The modern Olympics have an especially dark but little-known history. In preparation for the 1936 Olympics, the Nazis ruthlessly purged homeless people and slum-dwellers from areas of Berlin likely to be seen by international visitors. While subsequent Olympics–including those in Mexico City, Athens, and Barcelona–were accompanied by urban renewal and evictions, the 1988 Seoul games were truly unprecedented in the scale of the official crackdown on poor homeowners, squatters and tenants; as many as 720,000 people were relocated in Seoul and Injon, leading a Catholic NGO to claim that South Korea vied with South

Recent articles support Davis's generalizations. In an article entitled "UN Accuses Brazil of Displacing People by Force Because of World Cup and Olympics," the author describes how favelados in São Paulo, Rio de Janeiro, Belo Horizonte, Curitiba, Porto Alegre, Recife, Natal, and Fortaleza were removed from their homes in 2011 because of the upcoming games in a manner that might be considered a violation of human rights.[51] An article from 2012 titled "Residents Lose Homes Because of Cable Car in Favela in Rio," describes how buildings in the oldest favela in Rio were being demolished to make way for a cable car (part of a larger urbanization project connected with the World Cup).[52] The increased risk of removal may be due to numerous factors. Increased real estate prices might lead land owners and developers to build on the land where favelas are currently located. The games might provide the popular support for and the momentum necessary to enact removal policies that may have been harder to carry out under different circumstances.

Rio de Janeiro favelas have recently been in the news due to the Força de Pacificação (Pacification Force) campaigns carried out by the Brazilian army and military police in Rio de Janeiro's favelas since the end of 2008.[53]

Africa as "the country in which eviction by force is most brutal and inhuman." Beijing seems to be following the Seoul precedent in its preparations for the 2008 Games: "350,000 people will be resettled to make way for stadium construction alone." Human Rights Watch has drawn attention to extensive collusion between official planners and developers, who manipulate the patriotic excitement inherent to the Olympics in order to justify mass evictions and selfish landgrabs in the heart of Beijing."

51. "ONU acusa Brasil de desalojar pessoas à força por conta da Copa e Olimpíada," O Estado de São Paulo, April 26, 2011.

52. Silvana Bahia, "Palanque BBC: Moradores perdem casas com teleférico em favela do Rio," BBC Brasil, accessed October 10, 2012.

53. "Sem UPP, algum resquício de tráfico permanece no Alemão, diz ONG," Radio EstadãoESPN, accessed October 15, 2012. "Pacificação" or

The official objective of the pacification campaigns is to restore security to spaces once governed by armed criminals and drug dealing gangs. Rio's state government intensified the pacification process of certain favelas in response to the attacks on public buses by the drug gangs Comando Vermelho and Amigos dos Amigos in November 2010.[54] Since 2008, the state government has set up Unidades de Polícia Pacificadora (Pacification Police Units or UPPs) in thirteen favelas and aims at establishing another twenty-seven UPPs by 2014.[55] Since the pacification campaign intensified, violent crime and property crime have fallen in Rio, perhaps because criminals have been deprived of the protection previously found in favelas.[56] In fact, many residents of Rio see recent events as "a turning point for a city which has suffered decades of misgovernment."[57] Yet the benefits of pacification come hand in hand with issues such as police corruption, human rights violations, and the potential increased power of militias in favelas.[58]

"pacification" is used to describe the program implemented by Rio de Janeiro's Secretary of Public Security José Mariano Beltrame and Governor Sérgio Cabral that aims to establish police control of favelas controlled by drug dealers.

54. Ibid.

55. "Conquering Complexo do Alemão[:] A Big Step Towards Reclaiming Rio de Janeiro from the Drug Dealers," *The Economist*, December 2, 2010.

56. H.J., "Rio de Janeiro[:] Hoping for the Best; Preparing for the Worst," *The Economist*, January 3, 2011.

57. "Conquering Complexo do Alemão[:] http://www.economist.com/node/ 17627963.

58. "Eike Batista[,] The salesman of Brazil[:] Brazil's richest man is betting on resources and infrastructure. Can he deliver?" *The Economist*, May 26, 2012, http://www.economist.com/node/21555907. According to this article, Eike Batista provided millions of dollars to equip police in Rio's favelas.

FAVELAS IN BRAZILIAN CULTURE

Fernando Cavallieri noted that in the late 1970s and early 1980s, members of the Prefeitura do Rio de Janeiro, in an attempt to be politically correct, began referring to favelas as *aglomerações de baixa renda* (low-income agglomerations). Citizen groups, including those representing Rio's favelas, advocated that the term favela should be used because this was the word used and accepted by the general population, favelados, and favela community leaders. "Even if it is still used with a depreciative connotation," Cavallieri stated, the word favela "is also the affirmation of an identity."[59]

Most recently, after years of expressing discomfort with Google's inclusion of the city's favelas in its maps, Rio's municipal government recently requested that the digital mapping service display certain favelas less prominently, omit labeling of others altogether, and replace the word favela with *morro*, meaning "hill" in Portuguese. Morro is often used as a synonym for favela in Brazil, but is less recognizable to foreigners who will be examining maps of the city in preparation for the World Cup and Olympic Games. This is yet another recent example of how favelas are consciously rendered invisible by government officials who consider them to be backwards and unsightly and therefore in need of being hidden or removed.[60]

59. Fernando Cavallieri, "Favelas no Rio: a importância da informação para as políticas públicas" (paper presented at the O que é a favela, afinal? conference, Maré, Rio de Janeiro, August 19-20, 2009).
60. "A Pedido da Prefeitura, Google faz remoção virtual no mapa do Rio de Janeiro," website of the Comitê Popular Rio Copa & Olimpíadas, April 7, 2013, http://comitepopulario.wordpress.com/2013/04/07/a-pedido-da-prefeitura-google-faz-remocao-virtual-no-mapa-do-rio-de-janeiro/. See also Barnes, Taylor. "Rio's Shantytowns Shrink–on Google Maps, at Least," *The Christian Science Monitor*, April 27, 2011, http://www.csmonitor.com/

Favelas are stigmatized territories within cities, considered safe havens for criminals, and excluded from state protection.[61] Many well-organized, well-connected drug gangs and networks are based in and operate out of Brazilian favelas.[62] As a result, favelas are perceived simultaneously as home to millions of powerless Brazilians who live in poverty and drug dealers with easy access to sophisticated weaponry, independent militias, and vigilante groups who can kill at will. Brazilian mass media, which can be described as sensationalist when the subject is the country's favelas, foment fear to justify police brutality. In doing so, the media often capitalize on existing stereotypes instead of highlighting the Brazilian government's indifference to the rule of law and the actions of underpaid, understaffed, and unaccountable police forces.[63]

Academics, sociologists, and journalists, among others, disagree on how to depict the relationship between favelas and Brazil's formal cities. Mike Davis, for example, argues that metropolitan space has been fundamentally reorganized in a manner that is a "return to the medieval city" in which the "implications of middle-class secession from public space–as well as from any vestige of a shared civic life with the poor–are more radical."[64] Davis believes that the lives of rich and poor

World/Americas/2011/0427/Rio-s-shantytowns-shrink-on-Google-Maps-at-least/%28page%29/2

61. Nicole Maria Turcheti E. Melo, "Public policy for the favelas in Rio de Janeiro: the problem (in) framing" (M.A. diss., International Institute of Social Studies, Erasmus University, Rotterdam, 2010), accessed October 12, 2012, http://hdl.handle.net/2105/8698.

62. Gerônimo Leitão, "Quem conhece uma favela, conhece todas?" (paper presented at the O que é a favela, afinal? conference, Maré, Rio de Janeiro, August 19-20, 2009).

63. Perlman, 3004-07, 3339-45.

64. Davis, 2679-83.

Brazilians intersect less often today than they did in the past because situations that "transcend traditional social segregation and urban fragmentation" are less common.[65] The image of Brazilian cities as "divided" was furthered by Zuenir Ventura's *Cidade Partida* (*Divided City*). This 1994 book described Rio de Janeiro as a city at war, plagued by a form of apartheid; it argued that exclusionary policies aimed at the city's favelas proved to be disastrous.[66] Ventura shows how the city in the 1950s, idealized by many Brazilians as the golden age of Rio de Janeiro, already experienced social problems that would lead to the crime, divisions, and social tensions that would plague Rio in the 1990s.

Many challenge Ventura's description of Rio de Janeiro as a "divided city," arguing that, instead of separation, what actually prevails is inequality and discrimination. Favelados have been the source of labor in the richer areas of the city for decades.[67] The formal city and favelas have therefore always been interconnected in a systematic (albeit unequal) relationship. Perlman describes favelas as tightly integrated into the urban system, but notes that interactions between individuals are hierarchical and take place in "a perversely asymmetrical fashion."[68] Instead of characterizing the urban poor as "marginal" or irrelevant to the system, she argues that "favela residents contributed their labor, allegiance, and cultural wealth to the city—they built their communities, they built most of the rest of the city, and they voted as they were permitted,

65. Ibid.

66. Zuenir Ventura, *Cidade Partida* (São Paulo: Companhia das Letras, 1994), 11-14.

67. Maria Teresa Leal. Interview with author. Rio de Janeiro, Brazil, January 3, 2012.

68. Perlman, 254-59.

and in return they were excluded, exploited, and denigrated."[69]

✻✻✻

My hope is that, through an exploration of references to favelas in contemporary film, fashion, and furniture design, I can make the reader more aware of favelization's existence and stimulate a more dynamic debate about its potential impact. I do not intend to provide an exhaustive analyses of all situations in which references to favelas intersect with the luxury industry, nor is this a comprehensive study of contemporary Brazilian design. This book is an attempt to deepen discussions about ethics and design through an analysis of specific case studies, and to stimulate additional research about how producers of contemporary Brazilian culture are developing a vocabulary to market their products that raise important questions about ethics and social justice.

69. Ibid.

FAVELIZATION IN FILM

f the eyes are the window to the soul, film can be regarded as the window into Brazil's favelas. Film has become the means through which global consumers begin to "know" Brazilian favelas. Both fictional and documentary films represent the main source of images and information about favelas for Brazilian and non-Brazilian audiences alike. In fact, it is not uncommon to hear a non-Brazilian exclaim, "Oh yes, *City of God!*" when asked if she knows what a favela is. The case studies in this chapter challenge the representational role of two films, chosen from the numerous films about Brazil's favelas, poverty, and violence to have received international attention. I repeat here a question posed by other academics: Do films about favelas counter social exclusion or are they one of the mechanisms of its reproduction? In order to accurately describe the dynamics of favelization, one must start with film because it is the recent flood of movies, documentaries, TV series, and music videos that makes possible the marketing and branding language I will address in the subsequent chapters. Without internationally distributed films like *City of God* and, to a lesser extent, *Waste Land*, references to favelas would not trigger among consumers the images and associations they do today. The role of film in favelization is central.

It is worth digressing a moment to consider the "design" of film. Film is a manipulated, subjective medium, even when documentary. For example, what a filmmaker chooses to capture (and how) is as relevant as what she omits from a particular image, or what she declines to capture altogether. Images allow viewers exposure to spaces they may never experience first-hand. Yet film, even though it reproduces a visual experience of the otherwise unknown, is selected, assembled, and edited to compel a desired reaction in the viewer.[1] Filmmakers seek to design not only the images themselves, but also the perception of the viewer. Film is also a process made up of several types of design: interior design, lighting design, and costume design, aside from decisions of what to film, where to film, and what to exclude.[2] A number of different design decisions are made by filmmakers in order to further explicit or

1. John Tagg, *The Burden of Representation: Essays on Photographies and Histories* (Amherst: University of Massachusetts Press, 1988), 3. Tagg articulates how an image in and of itself does not communicate meaning. "The indexical nature of the photograph–the causative link between the pre-photographic referent and the sign–is therefore highly complex, irreversible, and can guarantee nothing at the level of meaning. What makes the link is a discriminatory technical, cultural and historical process in which particular optical and chemical devices are set to work to organize experience and desire and produce a new reality–the paper image which, through yet further processes, may become meaningful in all sorts of ways." An image of the favela on its own does not communicate meaning. A number of pre-existing referents, experiences, desires, and preconceptions are what together allow a viewer to interpret it.

2. John Walker, "Defining the Object of Study," *Design Reader* (Oxford: Berg Publishers, 2009), 42. Walker notes that the term "design" causes confusion "because it has more than one common meaning: it can refer to a process (the act or practice of designing); or the result of that process (a design, sketch, plan or model); or to the products manufactured with the aid of a design (designed goods); or to the look or overall pattern of a product ('I like the design of that dress')."

implicit political objectives. In other words, the manipulation of images influences the experience of viewing, and in doing so, films become a product with a designed outcome: a particular reaction of the viewer. Defining film as a designed process helps us understand how films about favelas both reflect and affect the relative distribution of power and authority over what favelas are.[3]

Films about Brazilian favelas can be compared to New Deal photography from the 1930s in the United States. Both have been regarded as documentary despite their promotional, political, or commercial agendas. During the Depression, photography played an important role in the United States as a record of the sacrifices endured by Americans. Yet despite "photography's apparent matter-of-factness," as noted by Pete Daniel and Sally Stein in *Official Images: New Deal Photography*, "photography contained contradictory impulses: to document and transform, to gain familiarity and distance.[4] Depression-era photography may seem to be a factual representation of what happened during the 1930s, but such photography was created to further a greater political objective. Despite their "documentary" candor and nonintrusive look, these pictures were governmental publicity aimed at promoting governmental intervention to stimulate the American economy.[5] This dual nature

3. Graham Bruce, "Alma Brasileira: Music in the Films of Glauber Rocha," *Brazilian Cinema*, eds. Randal Johnson and Robert Stam (Austin, TX: University of Texas Press, 1988), 291, citing an interview with Glauber Rocha in Image et Son 236 (February 1970). In this sense, film is similar to music: A song is designed but the experience of the song is the final product.

4. Pete Daniel, Merry A. Foresta, Maren Stange, and Sally Stein, *Official Images: New Deal Photography* (Washington, DC: Smithsonian Institution Press, 1987), viii.

5. Daniel, ix. As World War II "approached, the need for a yet more ideological

of New Deal photography–apparently documentary, but also promotional–is also manifest in contemporary film about favelas. A documentary style of presentation is often employed to further a project's authenticity and, therefore, authority. However, a promotional motive simultaneously exists, whether it is the desire to increase a film's commercial success or to augment an individual artist's visibility.

A discussion about the representation of favelas in film requires the recognition of two premises: that movies are commodities intended for consumption and at the same time are the products of the sociopolitical context in which they are made. Films about favelas are commodities intended to generate profit and exist within an industry (or industries) in which increasing sales is the primary objective. In "Slumsploitation: The Favela on Film and TV," Melanie Gilligan argues that:

> the internationally distributed Brazilian films we see today are products of increasingly commercial imperatives. All government-funded programmes supporting the Brazilian film industry were cut in 1991. Subsequently, the 'Audiovisual law' was created in 1993 to subsidise private investment in the film industry by granting Brazil's immensely wealthy corporations the right to invest up to 70 percent of their yearly income tax in film. The intention was to foster private investment in the film industry so that, when this initiative was phased out in 2003, corporations would continue financing films. The credits of

and abstracted industrial image became more pressing and constrained. In a famous memo, Stryker called in 1942 for photographs of 'people with a little spirit,' particularly 'young men and woman who work in our factories, [and] the young men who build our bridges, roads, dams and large factories."(Ibid., 4) Stryker's intention was to design photographs that, while seemingly authoritative because of their documentary style, furthered a larger political objective.

internationally exported Brazilian films such as *Lower City* or *City of God* list some of Brazil's biggest multinationals, for example Petrobras, many banks, and of course the monolithic Globo, who run 60 percent of national media. Unsurprisingly, the pressure to deliver high returns on investments ushered in an era of increasingly mainstream Americanised film-making in Brazil.[6]

While Gilligan focuses on the pressure for films themselves to generate profits, I would argue that the profit motive is broader depending on the film. Profit is the objective whether the film is a movie that generates box-office sales, a television commercial that increases the consumption of a product, or a music video that leads to song downloads, concert tours, and derivative sales of print media. A discussion of film therefore requires consideration of the filmic text, viewers' reception, aesthetics, and the nature of film's existence within a capitalistic market. The aesthetic of film is an important aspect of its market appeal and is, therefore, an important variable in the relationship between film as a product and the market for this product.

Film scholars Randal Johnson and Robert Stam argue that it is impossible to separate the filmic text from the social context in which it is made.[7] Therefore, films are a product of the social and political history of the places where they are made. In their book *Brazilian Cinema*, they

6. Melanie Gilligan, "Slumsploitation: The Favela on Film and TV," *Mute* 2, no. 3, 2006, http://www.metamute.org/editorial/articles/slumsploitation-favela-film-and-tv. See also Andre Gatti, "City of God: A Landmark in Brazilian Film Language," in *City of God in Several Voices: Brazilian Social Cinema as Action*, ed. Else R. P. Viera, Kindle edition, Highlight Loc. 1852-53. Gatti argues that "We may come to understand that the relationship between a product, its content and the aesthetics of a commodity with the market tends to become a variable that cannot be underestimated any more."

7. Randal Johnson and Robert Stam, eds., *Brazilian Cinema* (Austin, TX: University of Texas Press, 1988), 56.

state this is particularly the case in Brazilian film, where military rule, government censorship, and self-censorship led Brazilian filmmakers "to politicize their discussion of film to a degree that might surprise many non-Brazilians."[8] Brazilian cinema is not, for example, immune to class conflict–an important aspect of social relations in Brazil.[9] Brazilian and non-Brazilian filmmakers have incorporated their opinions, fears, and aspirations into their work about Brazil. Films such as *Waste Land* and *City of God*, in turn, reveal the legacy of stereotypical and fluid notions of Brazilianness, as well as the exaggerated perceptions of life in Brazilian favelas.

CAPTURING FAVELAS

Numerous contemporary movies include fly-over scenes of favelas. Else Viera, editor of *City of God in Several Voices: Brazilian Social Cinema as Action*, described this process as "catching Brazil," and argued these scenes show "these quintessential sites of exclusion, as if they were self-contained cities within the metropolitan sprawls of São Paulo and Rio [de Janeiro]."[10] Viera contends that sophisticated technology can "bring the real to the life of the screen" and render visible the reality of social exclusion "in its magnitude and diversity even for the eye that does not want to see."[11] This chapter questions the concept of "catching Brazil" by exploring images of favelas in the fictional film *City of God* (2002) and the documentary *Waste Land* (2011), two films that purport to "bring the real" of Rio de Janeiro's favelas to the screen. They are also hybrid projects, directed and produced by

8. Ibid.
9. Ibid., 10.
10. Viera, 409-13.
11. Ibid.

non-Brazilians with Brazilians who do not reside in favelas. Design is an important dimension of both movies. For example, by involving favelados in the filming process, their casting processes were designed to increase the believability of each story. The interiors of favela homes are either carefully recreated or selected for their emotional appeal. Furthermore, both *City of God* and *Waste Land* had as one of their objectives the transcendence by certain favelados of their realities through art. As such, they were designed to impact not only viewers but also the lives of those who participated in their making.

Waste Land and *City of God* offer millions of Brazilians and non-Brazilians visual access to favelas. While one is a documentary and the other fictional, both films merge social, ideological, and economic issues; aesthetic and artistic concerns; and cultural, historical, and anthropological themes.[12] Yet visual exposure to a space, even in a documentary, does not equal reality. A discussion of these two movies establishes a framework for a conversation about favelization in other types of design.

City of God and *Waste Land* were created for distribution inside and outside Brazil. Both received widespread media coverage internationally and were nominated for important international film awards. *City of God* recounts the story of a group of boys from an eponymous government-built housing development in Rio de Janeiro. The movie was directed by Fernando Meirelles and Kátia Lund and produced by O2 Filmes, Brazil's largest film production company and co-owned by Meirelles.[13]

12. Gatti, 1684-87.
13. See the City of God website http://cidadededeus.globo.com. See the Waste

Meirelles was involved in both *City of God* and *Waste Land* as a director in the prior and executive producer in the latter. He was born in 1955 to a middle-class family in São Paulo and studied architecture at the University of São Paulo. In the 1980s he began directing independent television series and then commercials in the 1990s. His filmmaking debut was in 1998 with *O Menino Maluquinho 2: A Aventura* and then *Domésticas* in 2000. By the time he began working on the script for *City of God*, Meirelles was the owner of Brazil's most successful advertising firm, O2, and one of the country's top advertising directors. Meirelles is a founder and director of O2 Filmes, a São Paulo-based production company established in 2001 that works on independent productions and co-productions with international studios and has worked on several projects related to Brazilian favelas.

Kátia Lund is a film director and screenwriter based in Brazil. She was born in 1966 in São Paulo to American parents who emigrated to Brazil before she was born. She attended the American Catholic school in São Paulo, Escola Maria Imaculada, prior to attending Brown University in Providence, Rhode Island. In fact, she is the middle daughter of two Americans who moved to São Paulo. According to *The Guardian*, Lund calls herself "bi-cultural" and "explains that the feeling of being an outsider helped her empathise with favela communities." Spike Lee hired Lund to work on the music video for Michael Jackson "They Don't Care About Us" which was filmed in the favela Dona Marta. Since then she has worked on several films related to favelas: the

Land website http://www.wastelandmovie.com/index.html. See also "Fernando Meirelles," http://www.imdb.com/name/nm0576987. See also the O2 Filmes website http://www.o2filmes.com/diretores/ fernando_meirelles.

documentary *Notícias de uma Guerra Particular (News of a Private War)*, *Golden Gate (Palace II)*, *City of Men*, and *All the Invisible Children*. Lund has also directed music videos for Brazilian and American hip-hop artists and was described by *The Guardian* in 2004 as "a film-maker specialising in Rio's most violent areas."[14]

The movie *City of God* is based on a fictional book published in 1997 by Paulo Lins titled *Cidade de Deus: Romance*. Lins grew up in Cidade de Deus and began writing the book while pursuing a degree in literature at the Universidade Federal do Rio de Janeiro. The book and movie show how, by the mid-1970s, City of God was home to gangs of teenage drug dealers, and by the mid-1980s it was plagued by gang warfare and conflicts between members of the drug trade and the police. The movie depicts a community in which murder is commonplace and few inhabitants are untouched by violence. *City of God* premiered at the 2002 Cannes Film Festival, after which it was nominated for numerous international awards, including four Oscars in 2004; according to the IMDB web-based film catalog, it has received over thirty international awards.[15]

City of God's creators used different types of design to create the impression of reality. As Lucia Nagib noted in "Talking Bullets: The Language of Violence in *City of God*," the film's "realist aspect" was created through a laborious process of production in which apparent

14. Alex Bellos, "And the winner isn't… Katia Lund co-directed the explosive City of God. Why was her name left off the Oscar nomination?" *The Guardian*, February 5, 2004, http://www.theguardian.com/film/2004/feb/ 06/oscars.oscars2004. Jean Oppenheimer, "Shooting the Real: Boys from Brazil," in *City of God in Several Voices: Brazilian Social Cinema as Action*, Highlight Loc. 1060-61.
15. "Awards for City of God," IMDB website, accessed on October 15, 2012, http://www.imdb.com/title/tt0317248/awards.

spontaneity is the result of "a considerable dose of artifice."[16] The types of "artifice" employed in the film included complex casting projects, detailed wardrobe development, and the strategic recreation of interiors. In sum, to recreate a high degree of realism, *City of God* became a hyperdesigned endeavor.[17] The documentary *Waste Land* captures the process through which artist Vik Muniz created a series of photographs in collaboration with garbage pickers in his native Brazil.Muniz was born into a working-class family in São Paulo in 1961. His father was a waiter and his mother a telephone operator. Muniz worked in advertising prior to moving to the United States at age 21 to learn English and study film. He stayed for seven years in the United States without returning to Brazil (because he was in the country illegally) and began his career in the visual arts, first as a sculptor, and then a photographer. He eventually spent two years in France, returning thereafter to New York. Muniz often works in series, using unexpected materials to recreate well-known artworks. His work is found in numerous public and private international collections. "My whole artistic formation took place in [New York]," states the now binational Muniz in his catalogue raisonné, and "that is why I consider myself an American artist. However, it is my sensibility as a Brazilian that enriches and differentiates this information." According to the artist, the "Pictures of Garbage" series shown in *Waste Land* marked "his return" to Brazil, where he now resides.[18]

16. Lucia Nagib, "Talking Bullets: The Language of Violence in City of God," *City of God in Several Voices: Brazilian Social Cinema as Action*, Highlight Loc. 1423-25.

17. Ibid., 1440-41.

18. Pedro Corrêa do Lago, *Vik Muniz: Obra Competa 1987-2009* (Rio de Janeiro: Capivara Editora Ltda., 2009), 27. See Muniz, *Lixo Extraordinário* (Rio de

Waste Land was a joint production of 02 Filmes (a São Paulo-based film company that also did *City of God*) and Almega Projects (a London-based production company). The documentary was co-directed by Lucy Walker from London, João Jardim from Rio de Janeiro, and Karen Harley from Pernambuco.[19] Walker, whom most press accounts give primary credit for directing the film, grew up in London and attended Oxford University. She won a Fulbright scholarship to pursue her MFA at New York University's graduate film program. In addition to *Waste Land*, Walker directed the documentaries *Countdown to Zero*, *Blindsight*, and *Devil's Playground*. The magazine *Salon* described Walker as a "charismatic and articulate Englishwoman who is well connected in the fields of film, art and fashion on both sides of the Atlantic."

Set primarily in Jardim Gramacho–the world's largest garbage dump, located in the outskirts of Rio de Janeiro–*Waste Land* exposes the work and private lives of individuals who search for recyclable materials that they redeem for money. In the movie, Muniz invites some of the trash pickers to pose for portraits and to work with him on large-scale artworks. The audience is led to believe all artworks created during the movie will be auctioned later in London at Phillips de Pury & Co. (now known only as Phillips) and the proceeds then donated

Janeiro: G. Ermakoff Casa Editorial, 2010), 157. See also "Muniz," Waste Land website, http://www.wastelandmovie.com/vik-muniz.html.

19. Luiz Zanin Oricchio, "Um filme, três autores: João Jardim fala da rotina de filmagem do documentário Lixo Extraordinário," O Estado de São Paulo, January 26, 2011, http://www.estadao.com.br/noticias/impresso,um-filmetres-autores,671106,0.htm. See Andrew O'Hehir, "Who Really Made the Oscar-nominated "Waste Land"? Unpacking the rumors around Lucy Walker's acclaimed garbage documentary," Salon, February 24, 2011, accessible at http://www.salon.com/2011/02/24/waste_land/. See also "Lucy Walker, Director," Waste Land website, http://www.wastelandmovie.com/lucy-walker.html.

to the trash pickers' cooperative. The movie's official website furthers this understanding by stating:

> One hundred percent of the sales from Vik Muniz's "Pictures of Garbage," the portraits of the catadores, as seen in the film, went back to the Association of Recycling Pickers of Jardim Gramacho (*Associação dos Catadores do Aterro Metropolitano de Jardim Gramacho*, or ACAMJG). Approximately USD \$250,000 was raised from the portraits….

However, auction records show that only one piece, entitled *Marat (Sebastião) Pictures of Garbage, 2008*, was actually sold at the June 29, 2008, Contemporary Art Evening Sale. It sold for £34,850.[20]

Waste Land shows images of favelas located near Jardim Gramacho, and in other parts of Rio de Janeiro. It was released in the United States in 2010, and then in the United Kingdom in 2011. *Waste Land* was nominated for

20. On the Phillips website, Marat (Sebastião) Pictures of Garbage, 2008, is listed as lot 272 of the Contemporary Art Evening Sale held in London on June 29, 2008. Text on the page states: "This is the only copy of an edition of two made available by the artist and the entire proceeds of its sale will benefit ACAMJ (Garbage Pickers Association of Jardim Gramacho) in the process of transition facing the imminent closing of the dump, an event that will affect 5.000 recycling workers and their families who derive their livelihood exclusively from the facility." In August 2013 I contacted Laura Gonzalez, the head of Latin American sales at Phillips, and Brooke de Ocampo, one of the auction house's International Specialists who appears in Waste Land alongside Muniz in his warehouse. I asked them over email whether all artworks created during the film were auctioned at Phillips in London or sold as private sales. I was unable to obtain information about whether pieces other than Marat were sold through Philips. It was also unclear whether any of the proceeds from the sales went towards Muniz's expenses in creating the film and artworks. "Lot 272," Phillips's website, accessed on August 23, 2013, http://www.phillips.com/detail/VIK-MUNIZ/UK010308/272.

Phillips's on-line auction records showing the artwork *Marat (Sebastião) Pictures of Garbage* (2008), Lot 272, auctioned at the Contemporary Art Evening Sale, June 29, 2008, London, UK. http://www.phillips.com/detail/VIK-MUNIZ/UK010308/272.

an Academy Award for Best Documentary in 2011, and an Outstanding Film Debut and Outstanding British Film at the British Academy Television & Television Craft Awards in 2011, among others.[21]

DESIGNING REALITY: AN IMPOSSIBILITY

Any attempt to portray reality in film–the "whole truth"–is impossible. By filming a favela one is automatically fragmenting its reality. The very act of filming is an act of deconstruction; the cohesion of lived experience is shattered into a collection of pictures.

21. Waste Land website, "Production Company," accessible at http://www.wastelandmovie.com/production-company.html and "Awards," accessible at http://www.wastelandmovie.com/awards.html.

Therefore, all visual materials created about favelas are merely images that capture shards of reality, not a total truth. Yet despite (or perhaps because of) this inherent limitation to filmmaking, "reality" is a recurrent theme in discussions about favelas, in film as in other types of design.

Film is the most popular source of images of favelas outside Brazil and perhaps second only to televised news in Brazil. Film has played a leading role in turning favelas into a popular image in global contemporary culture and is also the main instigator of a global fascination with favelas. In "The Fetish and the Favela: Notes on Tourism and the Commodification of Place in Rio de Janeiro, Brazil," Austin Zeiderman argued that:

> the favela, known through globally circulated cultural productions such as *City of God, Black Orpheus*, and the favela tour, represents to transnational consumers the city of Rio de Janeiro as a whole. Favelas are, in the global imagination, as synonymous with Rio as are the mountains, beaches, samba schools, and Carnival. As such, they are local productions, made for global consumption and circulation.[22]

Film acts as an avenue through which global consumers get to "know" favelas. The types of images films use to depict favelas or the lives of favelados vary. For example, some films highlight heart-wrenching aspects of favela life, others make it seem glamorous, and some use aspects

---

22. Austin Zeiderman, "The Fetish and the Favela: Notes on Tourism and the Commodification of Place in Rio de Janeiro, Brazil" (Lecture, Breslauer Graduate Student Symposium, University of California International and Area Studies, UC Berkeley, CA, April 14-15, 2006). Zeiderman argues that places are "produced for global circulation and consumption" in his discussion of a favela tour as a "site in which images of Rio de Janeiro are made for export." The author acknowledges the importance of film in the process of commodification of the favela and the globalized nature of the commodified images of the favela.

of Brazilian culture (such as Afro-Brazilian customs) to portray favelados as the primitive Other. As a whole, the existing films form an album of interpretations of these spaces: The act of image making has become a tool for shaping viewers' understanding of favelas. Images in films instruct the viewer on how to think and feel about favelas. However, most films about favelas are made by middle- or upper-class individuals who do not reside in these communities.

A HISTORICAL PERSPECTIVE OF FAVELA IN FILM

The history of favela in film reveals two trends: idealization of the life in favelas and attempted depictions of reality. The discussion below does not place the movies cited in their full historical context; the examples below indicate that favelization is not a novel phenomenon. Since the early 1900s, movies have romanticized favelas as a source for, among many things, hedonistic pleasure, talented soccer players, and samba music.[23] For example, in *Black Orpheus* (1959), French director Marcel Camus created an idealized image of favela life through the film's focus on Carnival, samba school pageants and music, with a subplot of a love story based on the Greek myth of Orpheus and Eurydice.[24] Viera described the film's favelas as a "world full of passion" where "solidarity seems to fill the vacuum of racial politics," and argued that *Black Orpheus* "eroticizes the black population" by portraying

23. Viera, 425-33.
24. Robert Stam, *Tropical Multiculturalism: A Comparative History of Race in Brazilian Cinema & Culture* (Durham, NC: Duke University Press, 1997), 167, 170. Stam notes that Black Orpheus is often regarded as a Franco-Brazilian collaboration given that it was based on a play by Brazilian playwright Vinícius de Moraes, features Brazilian music, Brazilian actors, Brazilian samba performers, and Brazilian film technicians; only four crew members were French.

blacks erroneously as a minority in Brazil.[25] Stam furthers Viera's analyses by stating that *Black Orpheus* romanticizes the favela despite Camus and his screenwriter's having spent five months in Rio de Janeiro's favelas conducting research (an experience that might have translated into a more restrained use of stereotypes). Stam notes that the movie forged "in the international consciousness a powerful association between three related concepts: Brazilianness, blackness, and carnival."[26] As both *Waste Land* and *City of God* do for contemporary audiences, *Black Orpheus* initiated millions of non-Brazilians into Brazilian culture.[27]

On the other hand, some movies represent attempts to depict favelas' reality(ies). The idea that filmmakers can record reality is recurrent in the history of cinematic depictions of Brazilian themes. Like Camus, Humberto Mauro spent time in Rio de Janeiro favelas to learn about the everyday life and songs of its inhabitants for his movie *Favela dos Meus Amores* (*Favela of My Loves*, 1934).[28] Mauro described his work as an attempt to record fact: "I simply grabbed life in the favelas as it was. I documented it."[29] In fact, Stam notes that when Mauro was asked if he saw himself as a precursor of neorealism, Mauro replied: "What is Neo-Realism? Isn't it simply realism?"[30] The notion that film (even those that are not journalistic) can grab favela life and document it in a manner that is "realistic" prevails in discussions of movies like *Waste Land* and *City of God*.

Despite the long history of favelization in film, the

---

25. Viera, 586-91.
26. Stam, 167.
27. Ibid.
28. Johnson, 26.
29. Ibid.
30. Ibid.

inclusion of favelas in Brazilian and foreign films has increased significantly over the past two decades. Between 1934 and 1996, filmmakers released over forty-nine films, documentaries, TV series, and music videos that show favelas. Yet thirty-seven of them were released between 1996 and 2012.[31] The films show images of Brazilian favelas in varying degrees of proximity, detail, and aestheticized presentation. However, each film grants viewers virtual access to favelas. It is interesting to note that favelas has also become popular settings for video games (an area this chapter does not explore but deserves further research).

There are similarities between the depiction of favelas in some contemporary films and those attributed to the Cinema Novo movement, led by Brazilian filmmaker Glauber Rocha. In his 1965 manifesto, "An Esthetic of Hunger," Rocha advocated for Brazilian filmmakers to abandon the glamour common in Hollywood film during the 1960s in favor of films having "a gritty social and political orientation."[32] Rocha defined Cinema Novo as "not one film but an evolving complex of films that will ultimately make the public aware of its own misery."[33] This type of cinema was to be inherently political: the movies were to further the freedom of Latin America from colonialism, imperialism, and economic dependence. In "An Esthetic of Hunger," Rocha called upon filmmakers of any age and background to "film the truth and oppose the hypocrisy and repression of intellectual censorship" and to dedicate their professional lives to "the great causes of our time."[34]

31. See http://favelization.net/film/
32. Viera, 382-86.
33. Glauber Rocha, "An Esthetic of Hunger," *Brazilian Cinema* 71.
34. Ibid., 70.

According to Johnson and Stam, Cinema Novo movies were made during a phase of cultural renewal in Brazil that began in the early 1950s and gained momentum with the election of Juscelino Kubitschek as president in 1955.[35] These movies were, according to Rocha, "sad, ugly... screaming, desperate films."[36] Kubitschek's administration fanned nationalist sentiment and supported economic policy that fostered foreign investment in Brazil.[37] Cinema Novo films were made during a period described by Johnson and Stam as one of "apparent economic expansion based on foreign investment, a period of political militancy, strong nationalist sentiments, and increasing social polarizations."[38] To a certain extent, many contemporary films about favelas, including *City of God* and *Waste Land*, echo some of the principles set forth by Rocha, since they tell the stories of some of the great causes of our time: poverty and crime. It is also worth mentioning that what Rocha called "gritty" is now glamorous and described by Gilligan as "a now formulaic MTV-povera aesthetic." The favelization of today is a fascinating synthesis of the grit Rocha wanted to portray and the glamour he wanted to eschew.

However, the fundamental political difference between Cinema Novo movies and *City of God* and *Waste Land* is politics. Rocha was against Brazilian cultural products that distorted political issues, "especially the formal exoticism that vulgarizes social problems."[39] He contended that such products provoke "a series of

35. Johnson and Stam, 30.
36. Rocha, 70
37. Johnson and Stam, 30.
38. Ibid.
39. Rocha, 69.

misunderstandings that involve not only art but also politics."[40] *City of God* and *Waste Land* present social issues in a problematic manner: the former in a highly aestheticized and hyperdesigned visual style, the latter through a depiction of the trash pickers' lives with the intent to promote Muniz's career and work. While attempting to recreate reality, both movies overdramatize and oversimplify the social, economic, and political issues related to favelas. The result is commercial products that exoticize and vulgarize social problems.

Rocha would likely also denounce the commercial nature of *City of God* and *Waste Land*. Both films are commercial ventures and were distributed through international commercial channels. So while *City of God* and *Waste Land* extensively document issues related to poverty, they were created in and established for international commercial networks of distribution and consumption. Cinema Novo was to operate separately from the commercial film industry. Throughout Brazilian cinematic history, discussions have often been tainted with what Johnson and Stam described as "inadvertent leftist condescension" of the type of which Rocha may be accused.[41] While the politicized standards of Cinema Novo do not represent a benchmark of quality for all cinematic production, they are a useful departure point for questioning a film's commercial objectives.

City of God and *Waste Land* were created by individuals privy to the economic and global dimension of the international film industry. Both Meirelles and Muniz, for example, had experience working in advertising and commercial film. The movies were made for an international audience by individuals with a keen

40. Ibid.
41. Stam, 164.

understanding of the circulation of a broad range of visual materials and images of Brazil in the contemporary world. As Andre Gatti notes in "*City of God*: A Landmark in Brazilian Film Language," certain movies evidence "the ability of some Brazilian film-makers to tune into the contemporary international project of circulation of audio-visual material."[42] Given the return-on-equity requirements for a commercial movie, it would follow that the depiction of favelas in them would be crafted to appeal to the tastes of international audiences, and that expectations regarding markets would influence the way in which social, economic, and political issues are treated (e.g., the less political the presentation of the issues related to favelas, the more palatable the film is to a broader audience). Favelization often involves situations in which non-Brazilians and middle- or upper-class Brazilians, with high levels of expertise in a given field, control the depiction of favelas and use its reality for personal benefit.

Contemporary films depicting favelas have been labeled "neo-favela", a new genre that usually combines images of favelas with violence and contemporary Brazilian music. Neo-favela films present social issues like crime and poverty alongside what Viera described as "a place full of colour, ubiquitous music and weekly balls."[43] In other words, socioeconomic issues are presented but glamorized or balanced with aestheticized, entertaining, or even erotic images. Neo-favela clashes with Rocha's standards for Cinema Novo: The movement's movies were to show social issues that "will not be cured by moderate governmental reforms and that the cloak of Technicolor cannot hide."[44] Rocha did not

42. Gatti, 1742-45.
43. Viera, 425-33.

want his films to suggest the issues portrayed could be quickly fixed; nor did he glamorize them. Although modern film technology has surpassed Technicolor, *City of God* represents the landmark film of the neo-favela style not only because of its immense international success, but also because of its noteworthy use of color, filming techniques, sound, and violence. Similarly, Muniz's striking artworks obfuscate the greater issues at play in the context in which they were made. Furthermore, *Waste Land* seems to suggest, in an excessively simplistic manner, that poor people's lives can be easily transformed by capable and visionary individuals.

INTERPRETATION, TRANSCENDENCE, AND DOMINATION

Both *City of God* and *Waste Land* introduce a triad of attributes typical of favelization: interpretation, transcendence, and domination. Interpretation refers to the role of non-favelados as intermediaries for favelas and their realities. Through film—more precisely, the design of their films—filmmakers act as the active interlocutors between the passive favela and film viewers.

Favelas in these movies are what John Tagg describes as a feminized Other and object of knowledge, "[s]ubjected to a scrutinising gaze, forced to emit signs, yet cut off from command of meaning." Throughout history, "the working classes, colonized peoples, the criminal, poor, ill-housed, sick or insane were constituted as the passive" and "pathetic objects capable only of offering themselves up to a benevolent, transcendent gaze—the gaze of the camera and the gaze of the paternal state."[45]

44. Rocha, 70.
45. Tagg, 11-12.

The very act of photographing or filming, according to Tagg, inscribes relations of power into the interpretation, creating a paternalistic relation of domination and subordination. Whether purporting to be documentary or fictional, many depictions of favelas involve distortion, bias, and cooptation.[46]

Transcendence is the objective of the philanthropic projects created in connection with *City of God* and *Waste Land*. Through their participation in these projects, favelados are expected to transcend the challenges of life in favelas. Transcendence is often stated as an objective in films themselves, the written materials produced about the films, interviews, and articles written about the movies. The *New York Times*, for example, noted that Muniz

> has a mystical faith in the artistic power of transformation, as one thing becomes another and garbage is turned into art. He fervently believes that he is changing his subjects' lives for the better by "showing them another place," even if they never make it out of Jardim Gramacho.[47]

46. Ibid., 12. "Documentary photography traded on the status of the official document as proof and inscribed relations of power in representation which were structured like those of earlier practices of photo-documentation: both speaking to those with relative power about those positioned as lacking, as the 'feminised' Other, as passive but pathetic objects capable only of offering themselves up to a benevolent, transcendent gaze–the gaze of the camera and the gaze of the paternal state. But in its mode of address, documentary transformed the flat rhetoric of evidence into an emotionalised drama of experience that worked to effect an imaginary identification of viewer and image, reader and representation, which would suppress difference and seal them into the paternalistic relations of domination and subordination on which documentary's truth effects depended."

47. Stephen Holden, "From a Universe of Trash, Recycling Art and Hope," The New York Times, October 28, 2010, http://movies.nytimes.com/2010/10/29/movies/29waste.html

It is entirely possible that Muniz believes in the transformative impact of this project. However, transcendence is not synonymous with sustainable change. We must therefore ask: Does the temporary nature of the film's philanthropic projects, the salaries earned while working on the movies, and even the skills accrued during these experiences amount to sustained improvement in the lives of most participants? Is it possible that instead of transcendence, these projects often generate a temporary escape from the challenges of favela life, not a release from poverty? It is a fact that the organization created during *City of God* to train actors remains active today as an independent nongovernmental organization. Is it an example of how the theme of transcendence can be turned into a sustainable reality?

Domination is the result of the unequal power dynamics between filmmakers and who or what is filmed in favelas. Certain types of favela representation might be designed to satisfy a foreign market that Rocha described as "nostalgic for primitivism."[48] A fundamental question related to favelization and film is: Who dominates the narrative of favelas and mediates the demand for the exotic? By controlling the depiction of a generalized favela, films dominate the public narrative of these communities. *City of God* and *Waste Land* were produced by nonfavela dwellers who curated (selected, organized, and presented) the stories told in the film and, in doing so, controlled the storytelling.[49] Additionally, transcendence

---

48. Rocha, 69.

49. Ibid. Rocha wrote: "Thus, while Latin America laments its general misery, the foreign onlooker cultivates the taste of that misery, not as a tragic symptom, but merely as an esthetic object within his field of interest. The Latin American neither communicates his real misery to the 'civilized'

is often only made possible (and realized) in films like *City of God* and *Waste Land* thanks to the "guidance" of nonfavelados. These ostensibly benevolent interventions are actually a form of domination.

WASTE LAND

Waste Land includes approximately seven scenes of the Jardim Gramacho favela located in the largest trash dump of the state of Rio de Janeiro. The first scene consists of aerial pictures taken by Muniz and his team during a helicopter ride over Jardim Gramacho. A dialogue between Muniz and his assistant, Fabio Ghivelder, and music by Moby accompany the slideshow of the landfill and the adjacent favela. While analyzing the aesthetic qualities of different images (given they were taken for use in artwork), Muniz also discusses the level of poverty he sees and the marginalization of that favela. He states, "It's good to fly over so we can see what we're up against. It's like this all over. Look at this. This is by far the worst I've seen. It looks like they were completely left (sic)." The images chosen, the music, and the dialogue interpret that favela for the viewer. The conversation between Muniz and Ghivelder is designed to facilitate the viewer's understanding of the images but it is a conversation between a stylized, filmmaker-curated, symbol of favelas and the viewer.

The images contextualize Muniz's larger endeavor and educate viewers as to the size, location, and conditions of Jardim Gramacho. Together with the dialogue and the music, they form an interpretation of favela life in Jardim Gramacho that echoes the perceived otherness of

European, nor does the European truly comprehend the misery of the Latin American."

Poster. *Waste Land,* 2010.

the favela ("what we're up against"), and the favelados' need for guidance and transcendence ("the worse I've seen" and "they were completely left"). The scene, with its emphasis on aerial images that make Jardim Gramacho somehow comprehensible and manageable, helps explain and justify Muniz's intervention and domination. The flyover images of Jardim Gramacho and the voice-over are used to show the viewer what is "at stake" in Muniz's project. In *When the Moon Waxes Red: Representation, Gender and Cultural Politics,* Trinh T. Minh-Ha describes the multiple types of domination that take place in documentary scenes:

The socially oriented filmmaker is thus the almighty voice-giver (here, in a vocalizing context that is all-male), whose position of authority in the production of meaning continues to go unchallenged, skillfully masked as it is by its righteous mission. The relationship between mediator and medium or, the mediating activity, is either ignored–that is, assumed to be transparent, as value free and as insentient as an instrument of reproduction ought to be–or else, it is treated most conveniently: by humanizing the gathering of evidence so as to further the status quo.[50]

Muniz's interpretation of the images is in no way neutral: it relates to his greater objective (to carry out an aesthetic project of his own) and reinforces pre-existing power dynamics.

Vik Muniz at Jardim Gramacho. Photograph by Fabio Ghivelder. Courtesy of Vik Muniz Studio.

Images of poverty heighten the viewer's emotional response to the story being told. Although aerial shots are effective, scenes of favela home interiors provoke the strongest reactions, allowing viewers to compare their private lives (assumed to be better) with those of the movie's subjects. In two separate *Waste Land* scenes, the

50. Trinh T. Minh-Ha, *When the Moon Waxes Red: Representation, Gender and Cultural Politics* (New York: Routledge, 1991), 36.

trash picker Suelem shows viewers her living quarters near the landfill and then her mother's home (where Suelem's children live). Suelem narrates both scenes, explaining to the viewers what they are seeing, how the spaces function, and who is shown in the spaces.

The small, one-bedroom *barraco* Suelem rents in the Jardim Gramacho favela is cramped, dirty, and rat-infested. The roof leaks when it rains, and the door leads to an unpaved alley that is covered in trash.

Screen shot. Suelem looks down the alley near the home she rents during a scene in *Waste Land*, 2010. Courtesy of Almega Projects.

Suelem's mother's house is also a barraco. The walls are dark (perhaps because they are made of unfinished plywood or cement), and the interior looks dirty and unkempt. Suelem leads the camera around her mother's home, describing each part of her mother's barraco. The living room, for example, doubles as a bedroom for several family members.

Such scenes show housing that is impermanent, dirty, and disorganized, stereotypes often tied to poverty. I believe such images are used to evoke pity. *Waste Land* presents these interiors as representative of the reality of the other characters in the movie–even though the homes of other garbage pickers (which are cleaner and less precarious) are also included in the film, albeit in narrower angles and in shorter scenes. These two scenes focused on Suelem's dwellings serve two functions: to inspire the feelings of pity and empathy in viewers, and to create an image of decay that counters the beauty created in the art project led by Muniz.

Screen shot. Vik Muniz takes a photo of Tião as Marat (screen grab). Courtesy of Vik Muniz Studio.

View of Irmã's portrait being assembled in Vik Muniz's Rio de Janeiro studio. Photograph by Vik Muniz. Courtesy of Vik Muniz Studio.

Waste Land's overarching theme is that art can transform lives. The scenes of Suelem's living conditions are used to portray the "ugliness" of favela life and the trash pickers' lives before their experiences with Muniz. This ugliness is then contrasted with the beauty of the artwork created through Muniz's intervention and the spaces to which the trash pickers gain access as a result of their relationship to Muniz. Because of the project, for example, the trash pickers attend an art opening at the Museu de Arte Moderna in Rio de Janeiro, and one of the trash pickers gets to attend an auction in London. The contrast between the interiors of the barracos and the landfill, and the museum and London further the notion of transcendence in *Waste Land*. The garbage pickers, who live in favelas, transcend their reality by working with Muniz. The climax of this transcendence is the scene in which artwork from the project is auctioned at Phillips de Pury & Co. in London. The scenes connected to the auction depict stark, predominantly white, clean, modern interiors–the diametric opposite of the scenes of the Jardim Gramacho favela.

The themes of interpretation and transcendence in *Waste Land* are connected to the issues of guidance and domination. The documentary interprets a favela by photographing, filming, and describing it. The agents of transcendence and guidance are individuals who do not live in favelas (Muniz, Ghivelder, and the film's directors, for example). The film shows how Muniz ushers the garbage pickers through an artistic process that is supposed to improve their personal lives.

The contrast between the interiors (dark and dirty to white and clean) is one way in which the film makes the intended transformation visible. But what is the ideology

Magna. Photograph by Vik Muniz.
Courtesy of Vik Muniz Studio.

behind this desire to enable transcendence? In *Wasted Lives: Modernity and its Outcasts*, Zygmunt Bauman describes the bias that underlies the desire to dominate and change. "There are always too many of them. 'Them' are the fellows of whom there should be fewer–or better still none at all. And there are never enough of us. 'Us' are the folks of whom there should be more."[51] Transcendence may be the means through which uncomfortable social issues and differences become sanitized, manageable, and eventually nonexistent. It might be the way in which a dominant group can create

51. Zygmunt Bauman, *Wasted Lives: Modernity and its Outcasts* (Stafford, Australia: Polity Press, 2004), 34.

Final Magna photographic print entitled
The Gipsy Magna–Pictures of Garbage.
Photograph by Vik Muniz. Courtesy of
Vik Muniz Studio.

more of what Bauman describes as "us," and less of
"them."

CITY OF GOD

City of God's creators employed a significant amount of
artifice to create the impression of reality. As Lucia Nagib
noted in "Talking Bullets: The Language of Violence in
City of God," the film's realist aspect was created through
a laborious process of production in which apparent
spontaneity is the result of "a considerable dose of
artifice."[52] Significant effort was invested in the casting,
costume design, and recreation of interiors featured in

Vik Muniz and Magna in Jardim Gramacho. Photograph by Fabio Ghivelder. Courtesy of Vik Muniz Studio.

the film to create an impression of authenticity. As a result, *City of God* became an example of how interpretation can also be a matter of hyperdesign.[53] This is particularly problematic given that *City of God* became the reference for most Brazilians and non-Brazilians, who believe it is realistic and a pseudojournalistic account of favela life.

City of God's casting process is an example of artifice employed as a means of enhancing the film's realism. Despite the fact that a significant percentage of Brazilians are black, the country's actors are predominantly white. As Meirelles was unable to identify a sufficient number of actors for the film, he created a complex casting and training program. The press releases and interviews about *City of God* describe how Meirelles personally financed not just the filming of the movie, but also the

52. Nagib, 1423-25.
53. Ibid. 1440-41.

Poster. *City of God*, 2002.

long, labor-intensive, and expensive casting process that preceded it.[54] Meirelles is said to have invested almost three million dollars in the production of *City of God* and the lengthy series of workshops for child actors recruited from different favelas in Rio de Janeiro.[55]

To increase the visual veracity of *City of God*, Meirelles hired teenagers from favelas across Rio de Janeiro to act in the movie. In order to train them, the movie's production team created amateur theater schools in several Rio de Janeiro favelas, and interviewed two thousand potential actors.[56] Meirelles engaged Nos de Morro (Us from the Hill), a theater group run by Guti

54. Ibid., 1528-34.
55. Gatti, 1876-80.
56. Nagib, 1528-34.

Fraga, to assist in the process. This group is composed of residents of the favela Morro de Vidigal, and the group became responsible for training most of the actors in *City of God.* [57] Eventually, four hundred people were chosen to participate in workshops directed by Fraga. The workshops focused on improvisation exercises during which the teenagers were "observed and reported on by the directors and other members of the film's team."[58] Many of the movie's sixty main characters and the one hundred and fifty supporting cast members were selected through these workshops.[59]

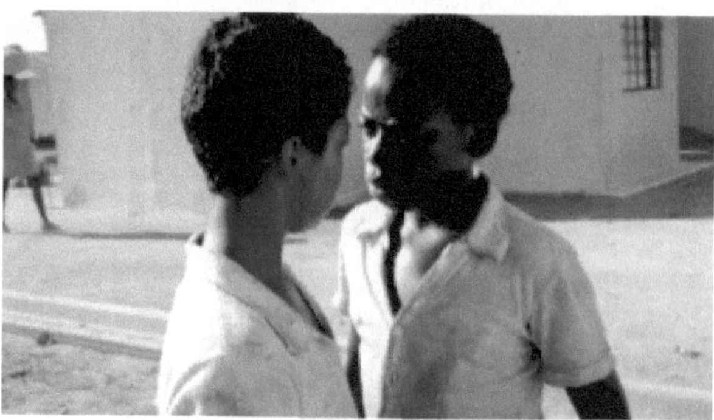

Screen shot. *City of God,* 2002.

Meirelles created the acting workshops to identify and train actors that could make *City of God* realistic. What is interesting about the film's casting process is that, even though Meirelles's intention was to create a process that would allow him to identify actors that matched his

57. Meirelles, 1060-61. See also Nós do Cinema website, http://www.dreamscanbe.org/view/338.
58. Nagib, 1528-34.
59. Alex Bellos, "And the winner isn't… Katia Lund co-directed the explosive City of God. Why was her name left off the Oscar nomination?" *The Guardian*, February 5, 2004, http://www.theguardian.com/film/2004/feb/06/oscars.oscars2004.

Screen shot. *City of God,* 2002.

interpretation of the favela, the casting process became an important educational process for the director. In "Writing the Script, Finding and Preparing the Actors," Meirelles describes how he learned about the lives of the favela dwellers he met during casting and through theater workshops. "After class, my conversations with these young men put me in touch with their reality," noted Meirelles, "the same reality of the film's characters."[60] Meirelles notes that these interactions led to a reevaluation of the script and the character's dialogue. The director states that the semester-long "learning experience" helped him prepare for the film he was going to make stating that "[e]verything was new... Those six months opened my eyes and I saw a Brazil I thought I already knew."[61] Meirelles's candid description of his experience reveals the disconnect between what he though he knew about the subject of the film and what he later learned.

The film was designed to visually read like a documentary. For example, it employed individuals from

60. Meirelles, 1098-1103.
61. Ibid.

the favela, used voice-over narration to help viewers interpret certain scenes, and, when access to real favelas proved difficult, it recreated favela-like interiors in a studio. While *City of God* is not a documentary, it is regarded by many as a window into Brazil's contemporary social ills. "*City of God* is not simply a film," argues Viera. "It is an important fact, a crucial event, a borehole in the conscience of the country."[62] Many Brazilians and non-Brazilians alike experienced the movie as a glimpse of Brazilian contemporary reality—an authoritative account of life in a Rio de Janeiro favela.

Screen shot. *City of God*, 2002.

Cesar Charlone, the movie's cinematographer, wanted the movie to resemble the documentaries made in Brazil at the beginning of the 1980s. To achieve that aesthetic, he used, for example, a handheld camera in order to "prevent even the minimum interference with reality."[63] By controlling the film's design, Charlone achieved the visual veracity he wanted.[64] In other words, to make the interpretation of favela life look realistic, significant

62. Viera, 174-75.
63. Gatti, 1796-1800.
64. Ibid.

Screen shot. *City of God*, 2002.

artifice was employed. Nowhere was the irony of this more relevant than in the case of the film's interiors; favela interiors were studio facsimiles, not actual favelas.[65] Most of the interior scenes in *City of God* were shot in studios.[66] While the filmmakers used natural light to illuminate all exterior shots during the day, location interiors were lit with practicals.[67] For example, in the scenes entitled "The Story of the Apartment" ("A História da Boca dos Apês"), viewers learn the history of an apartment used by different drug lords. The interiors of the apartments are aged, redecorated, and rearranged to show the passage of time. Different characters enter, inhabit, and leave the space in quick-cut scenes, and all the while, a narrator explains the changes that took place.

During these scenes, and indeed, during the entire film, the narrator assumes an authoritative stance towards the visual material depicted, explaining how things happened to the viewer. In *City of God*, design is the medium of

65. Meirelles, 1201-04.
66. Gatti, 1816-18.
67. Oppenheimer, 1340-42.

Screen shot. *City of God,* 2002.

Screen shot. *City of God,* 2002.

favela interpretation, and the narrator is an essential facilitator of this interpretation.

The narrator in *City of God* facilitates the domination of the favela. Although he represents a character in the movie from Cidade de Deus, the narrator speaks in formal Portuguese (different from the favela Portuguese spoken by most of the characters in the film) when he addresses the viewer. His role is to guide those who have never been to Cidade de Deus—or any favela—through three decades of history. He speaks for a reality most of

Screen shot. *City of God,* 2002.

Screen shot. *City of God,* 2002.

Cidade de Deus viewers have not experienced first-hand. Yet while the script he follows may have been based on Lins's experiences, the script was modified and adapted by the adapted by the filmmakers. The purported veracity of the story line, the authority inspired by the narrator, and the attention to the aesthetics of the film, resulted in a a movie that many believe to be extremely realistic. The film uses these techniques to achieve a position of reality regarding the favela—a common characteristic for movies that present their audience with something exotic. This exoticism is not incompatible with the filmmaker's intention to interpret the favela realistically; the documentary-like quality of the film is what made it exotic to both Brazilian and foreign audiences. Its exoticism was also an important factor in its global success.

CONCLUSION

Certain films about favelas, whether fictional or documentary, purport to show reality. They reflect filmmakers' belief that they can capture the life of Brazil's favelas. However, it is impossible to portray the whole truth through photography and film because artifice is employed by filmmakers to make films realistic. Numerous types of design are used to establish a sense of veracity (because when something seems real it therefore becomes authoritative and true). For example, certain interiors are shown because of their emotional appeal, scenes are edited so as reinforce notions of transformation, sound design is used to glamorize images, and authoritative voice overs are employed in order to guide the viewer's experience towards the intended interpretation. But all designed choices have consequences, not only for the movies themselves but for how audiences perceive the favelas.

What they do have is the power to idealize, glamorize or distort favela life. In purporting to document reality, certain movies overdramatize and oversimplify the social, economic, and political issues related to the favela. Unlike Cinema Novo movies, that focused primarily on politics, *City of God* and *Waste Land* exploit and vulgarize social problems in the process of creating a commercial product. These movies are made with the intention of maximizing box office sales or promoting the visibility of certain professionals. Despite their reputations as windows into the reality of Brazilian favelas, these movies are first and foremost commercial enterprises. While the idealism of Cinema Novo may not correspond with the reality of contemporary film industry, it creates a benchmark against which we can analyze examples of favelization. Furthermore, a discussion of favelas in film provides an essential framework for examining other types of design: the role of interpretation, transcendence, and domination.

FAVELIZATION IN FASHION

n 2009, the French polo shirt manufacturer Lacoste launched Campanas + Lacoste, a collaboration with Fernando and Humberto Campana, the designers described by *The New York Times* as "the Brazilian-born dynamic duo of design, who are renowned for their furniture creations made from discarded materials (and the odd stuffed animal)."[1] The Limited and Super Limited Edition shirts designed by the Campanas for Lacoste provide material for a case study of how luxury brands and designers are using references to Brazil's favelas to market contemporary luxury products. For the production of certain special edition shirts, Lacoste and the designers collaborated with the Cooperativa de Trabalho Artensanal e de Costura da Rocinha Ltda. (Coopa-Roca), a women's cooperative located in the Rio de Janeiro favela Rocinha. According to Coopa-Roca's website, its mission "is to provide conditions for its members, female residents of Rocinha, to work from home and thereby contribute to their family budget, without having to neglect their childcare and domestic duties. The work developed at Coopa-Roca has made it possible to improve the quality of life of the

1. "In-store: The Campana Brothers for Lacoste," *New York Times* (blog), Nov. 4, 2009, http://tmagazine.blogs.nytimes.com/2009/11/04/in-store-the-campana-brothers-for-lacoste/.

     Adriana Kertzer

craftswomen and, indirectly, also their families."[2] It is not a charity.

This chapter focuses on references to favelas in the marketing of luxury fashion.[3] Systemic socioeconomic issues in Brazil are being commodified, fetishized, misrepresented, and exploited by luxury brands in an attempt to add value and to market otherwise mundane objects as exotic. The Campanas + Lacoste shirts are an ideal case study because of how references to favelas were incorporated into their marketing. As the design critic Frederico Duarte noted in his thesis presentation "Beyond the Fruit Hat: Brazilian Product and Furniture Design Today," the advertising for Limited and Super Limited shirts dedicated a significant percentage of the language on the project's website to a description of who made the shirts.[4] I agree with Duarte's contention that the Campanas + Lacoste project's marketing focused more on the fact the shirts were made by women from a favela than it did on the fact that they were designed by well-known individuals. Duarte's observation has led me to explore in greater depth how this project turned certain spaces (favelas) and their inhabitants into an exotic Other for the purpose of promoting luxury products as "Brazilian."[5]

2. Coopa-Roca website, http://www.coopa-roca.org.br/.
3. Marco Romanelli, "Il disegno del mobile brasiliano: appunti di viaggio," *Domus* no. 728 (June 1991): 70.
4. Frederico Duarte, "Beyond the Fruit Hat: Brazilian Product and Furniture Design Today," (presentation, School of Visual Art's MFA Design Criticism symposium Crossing the Line: The 2010 D-Crit Conference, New York City, April 30,, 2010).
5. See Arjun Appadurai, *The Social Life of Things: Commodities in Cultural Perspective* (Cambridge, MA: Cambridge University Press, 1997).

SUMMARY OF THE CAMPANA BROTHERS' HISTORY

Fernando (b. 1961) and Humberto Campana (b. 1953) were born in Brotas, a small town in the countryside of the state of São Paulo.[6] They attended public school and came of age during the Brazilian military dictatorship.[7] During college, Humberto studied law, and Fernando pursued a degree in architecture.[8] Their collaboration as designers began in 1983/4 in São Paulo; the pair of iron chairs entitled Desconfortáveis (Uncomfortables) was one of their first joint projects.[9] The Campanas' work began to attract the attention of non-Brazilian media at the end of the 1980s. In a 1991 article, Marco Romanelli of the Italian magazine *Domus* described his findings from a trip to Brazil and featured the brothers' work prominently.[10] Other journalists, like Maria Tommasini and Francesca Picchi, praised their work as an alternative to a homogeneous view on design, defined by global models and high-tech, which was producing an unstoppable, all-conquering flood of bland industrial objects, insensitive to the specifics of geography or climate and indifferent to local traditions or concerns.[11] Over the years, the Campanas have received

6. Vik Muniz, "Campana Brothers," Bomb (Winter 2008), 2. See also Hannah Booth, "Waxing Brazilian," *Design Week*, Issue 19 (2004): 14-15. Accessible from http://bombsite.com/issues/102/articles/3040. See also Darrin Alfred et al., *Campana Brothers: Complete Works (So Far)* (New York: Rizzoli and Albion Gallery, 2010).

7. Muniz, 2.

8. Ibid., 2-3.

9. Irmãos Campana, *Cartas a um Jovem Designer: Do manual à indústria, a transfusão dos Campana* (Rio de Janeiro and São Paulo: Elsevier Editora, 2009), 75. See also Muniz, 2008, 3. The year noted as the beginning of the Campanas' collaboration in Muniz's article differs from the year stated in their autobiography, *Cartas a um Jovem Designer*. This text uses the year from the latter.

10. Romanelli 1991, 70.

significant attention in the design world for their humorous furniture, use of unexpected materials, international projects, and colorful designs.[12] They have also done product, interior, and stage design for numerous companies around the world.[13]

The Campanas' creations are examples of postmodern design often imbued with nationalist symbolism as defined by critics, journalists, and the designers themselves. When reading critics' description of the designers' work, one cannot help but wonder whether the authors project onto the Campanas a vision of what they want the designers to be (e.g., mediums of Brazilian culture, creators of distinctly "Brazilian" designs). Romanelli's article is an example of this transference:

> Their designs are a statement about the Brazil that really counts, the Brazil that rejects postmodernism and turns instead to its own, unique Le Corbusier and, with rather more nostalgia, to Lina Bo Bardi. This has resulted in a very different kind of design from the one we're used to. A design of compressed cardboard, junk wood, blow-moulded resins and lengths of plastic hose. [sic] These young masters with a difference come to the Milan Furniture Show every year, where they cheerfully do the rounds, keep their eyes peeled and tell you how much they've learned. Then they go back home and–thank goodness–send you an envelope a few months later containing photos of their new designs. You see burnt

11. aria Tommasini and Francesca Picchi, "Design Morbido./Soft Design," *Domus* no. 848 (2002) 118-23, as cited by Duarte, 2010.

12. Paola Antonelli, Projects 66: Campana / Maurer (New York: Museum of Modern Art, 1998) http://www.moma.org/interactives/exhibitions/1998/projects66/.

13. Campana, 58, 59, 60, 67, 68, 69, 70, 71, 72, 88, 96, 98, 147. See also the video clip of the anthropologist Dr. Ruth Cardoso discussing the dolls made by Artesanato Solidário and turned into a chair by the Campanas, http://youtu.be/Z0T5tIEAE_w.

charcoal, nylon thread, industrial mesh and twine, but their craft-based aesthetic also uses advanced technology (die-cast aluminum, for example). Their work is a mixture of past and future which, once again, makes it a portrait of today's Brazil.[14]

The Campanas' work does not visually resemble, even remotely, that of Le Corbusier. However, the Italian critic found it necessary to praise their creativity while also reading into their work familiar and canonical historical references. Romanelli's article, published ten years after the launch of Memphis (an aesthetic that could be characterized, in part, by its antihistoricism and antinationalism), seems to indicate a desire for the local, the national, and the exotic within postmodern production.[15] It is interesting that the Campanas mention the following designers as important influences: Danny Lane, Frank Gehry, Shiro Kuramata, Ron Arad, Ettore Sottsass, Andrea Branzi, Alessandro Mendini, Ingo Maurer, and Oscar Niemeyer.

The year 1998 marked an important turning point in the Campanas' careers. That year Paola Antonelli, the associate curator in the department of architecture and design at the Museum of Modern Art in New York, invited the Campanas to show their work at the museum. *Project 66*, an exhibition featuring the Campanas and the German lighting designer Ingo Maurer "catapulted [the Brazilian designers] into the center stage of international contemporary design."[16] The Campanas state in their autobiography that the international attention they received in 1998 was decisive in creating opportunities for the designers both outside Brazil and with Brazilian

14. Romanelli, 70.
15. Campana, 109.
16. Muniz, 2008, 2. See also "Campana Brothers," *Arts Review* 10 (2007): 90-93.

companies.[17] Since then, they have been perceived in the international market as "Brazilian designers" and are arguably the most famous designers from Brazil.[18]

The Campanas may be reluctant to identify themselves as ambassadors of Brazilian design, but they use Brazil as the "touchstone" for many projects.[19] They are among the world's most popular contemporary designers, and the fact that they are Brazilian is frequently highlighted in the media. In their autobiography, they state that "this connection with Brazilian culture is vital in our work."[20] "The Campana[s'] typical field of operations is the streets," noted *Interview Magazine.* "[T]hey're inspired by Brazil's make do culture and carnival spirit, and in their hands wood scraps, rubber hosing, fabric cast offs, old bottles and antennas become elegant, whimsical and thought-provoking chairs, tables and lighting."[21] Many of the Campanas' projects explicitly (because of their name) or indirectly (through the narrative used to describe them) relate to Brazil. They describe their sources of inspiration as their daily lives, where they live and the places they pass by during their daily routines in the city of São Paulo. They describe themselves as having "curious eyes, capable of seeing what really happens around us."[22] The designers themselves draw a comparison between the way in which they work and the manner in which favelados build their homes:

17. Campana, 57.

18. Muniz, 2008, 10.

19. Duarte, 2010.

20. Campana, 87.

21. Rebecca Voight, "The Campana Brothers Save Lacoste's Skin," *Interview Magazine* (blog), June 7, 2009, http://www.interviewmagazine.com/blogs/fashion/2009-07-06/campana-lacoste.

22. Campana, 85-86.

> [Our] project development is the same as that of the favelado who builds with what he has at hand, bringing from the most banal raw material, forgotten, a new function, without having to hide its origin. It is this strength of spirit making due with all the limitations, making with freedom. Who can align this with refined construction arrives at a universal product that is peculiarly Brazilian.[23]

This quote, like others, addresses the Campanas' active search for new ways of expressing Brazilian culture. However, many writers argue they paint "a portrait of their country,"[24] meaning that the Campanas' work is somehow representative of Brazilian reality, not merely inspired by it. The Campanas acknowledge the important role the media has played in their careers, and as they state in their autobiography, since the beginning of their careers they worried about "documenting and showing" their ideas. To what extent is their image as the ambassadors of Brazilian design self-manufactured? The Campanas describe their numerous lectures around the world in their autobiography: "In general, we deliver a summary of our experience, sometimes under the title The Spirit of Brazil: Transforming Chaos in (sic) Beauty, but trying to find new ways of exploring it, or else it becomes repetitive." This quote is interesting because it conflates their personal narrative with a title that explicitly connects them with nationalist ideas. Also revealing is the comment at the end of the same paragraph: "Today we feel great ease in speaking anywhere in the world, it seems even easier than in Brazil, where the perspective is more critical."[25]

One of the most well-known examples of favelization

---

23. Campana, 88.
24. Caroline Roux, "Interview: Campana Brothers," *Blueprint* 257 (2007) 54-57.
25. Campana, 124.

is the Campana Brothers' Favela Chair.[26] The Campanas say they made the original Favela Chair in 1991 from pieces of wood found on the streets of São Paulo.[27] The first chair was put together by the brothers themselves, but the manufacture of the chair in editions was initiated in 2003 by Edra, an Italian company. The Favela Chair today costs $4,685 and is made from new wood.[28] The Campanas explain in their autobiography that Edra's decision to manufacture the Favela Chair came after its owner (Massimo Morozzi) went with the Campanas to a favela that had been destroyed by fire.[29] The Campanas have created several products and projects related to the Favela Chair.

Despite the fact that the Favela Chairs by Edra are made in Italy and of new wood, some sources continue to market it by exaggerating its favela-ness.[30] For example, the Moss website–the gallery that represented the Campanas in the United States until 2012–stated:

> "Favela" refers to the ad-hoc shelters which are built out of mud, sand, scraps of wood, bricks and stones in the hills and on the fringes of urban expansion around Rio de Janeiro. The name refers to the location of the first of

26. "Fratelli Campana," *Abitare* 351 (1996): 204. See also Duarte, 2010.

27. Campana, 104. See also Duarte, 2010.

28. Duarte, 2010. Duarte noted that the original Favela Chair was put together by the Campanas themselves, but that it took Edra over ten years to figure out how to produce the design. Duarte recounts that Edra eventually subcontracted the manufacture of the chair to Habitart, a furniture company founded by German immigrants in southern Brazil. Each Favela chair is now made from hundreds of pieces of new wood, painstakingly assembled and, according to Duarte, with little room for improvisation. See Irmãos Campana, 104. See also Moss Gallery's website for the Favela Chair http://www.mossonline.com/product-exec/product_id/31681.

29. Campana, 110.

30. Ibid., 110.

"Favela Chair," 1991. Fernando and Humberto Campana. http://blog.sfmoma.org/2010/10/ darrin-alfred-favela-chair/

such settlements, the hill "Morro da Favela," built in the late 1800s by African-Brazilian veterans from the Canudos war who had nowhere else to go. The "Favela" chair is constructed piece-by-piece from the same wood used to build the favelas, and every piece is hand-glued and nailed.[31]

Moss stated on its website that the chair is made "from the same wood used to build favelas." This statement (which is not true) seems relevant enough to be listed on the store's website. Is this because the commodification and fetishization of favelas means that the mere mention

31. Moss Gallery website.

"Favela Chair," 2003. Fernando and Humberto Campana. Produced by Edra. http://www.edra.com/prodotto.php?id=24

of favelas in marketing materials helps increase a luxury item's emotional appeal?

Fernando and Humberto Campana building the Favela Mural at Moss Gallery in New York (December 2004). http://www.moss.coresense.com/ gallery-exec/display/campanas_gallery.

The Favela Chair is an example of how favelas have been commodified – how economic value is assigned to

"Favela Chair" in white marble, 2013. Fernando and Humberto Campana. Produced by Edra. http://www.edra.com/news.php?l=en.

"Vitra Miniature Favela Chair," 2009. Fernando and Humberto Campana. The Vitra Miniature Favela Chair was for sale on the MoMA Store's website (link is no longer active).

something not previously considered in economic terms.

Interior. "New Hotel," 2011. Fernando and Humberto Campana. Hotel is located in Athens, Greece. http://www.yatzer.com/NEW-Hotel-Campana-Brothers-Athens-Greece.

"Favela Bed," 2013. Fernando and Humberto Campana. Produced by Edra. http://www.dezeen.com/2013/04/15/campana-beds-by-fernando-and-humberto-campana-for-edra/?utm_source=feedburner&utm_medium=feed&utm_campaign=F

Some critics have praised the Favela Chair's design and

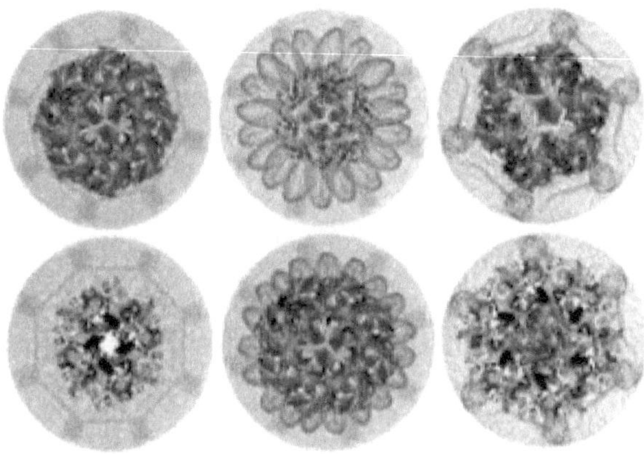

Plates. "Euro Tropiques" by Bernardaud, 2011. Fernando and Humberto Campana. Of the set of six plates, four plates have images of the Favela Chairs at the center. http://www.manorhg.com/store/images/BER_EuroTropiques_DinnerSet.jpg.

highlighted its "Brazilianness," describing it as an "homage to Brazilian ingenuity in the face of scarcity,"[32] a type of creativity others define as Brazil's "ultimate national trait."[33] Vik Muniz furthered this notion of Brazilianness during an interview with the Campanas by noting that "Brazilians pride themselves on repairing airplanes with paperclips, catching fish with prescription drugs as bait, or using saliva as a building material."[34]

32. Tommasini and Picchi, 118-23.
33. Duarte, 2010.
34. Muniz, 2008.

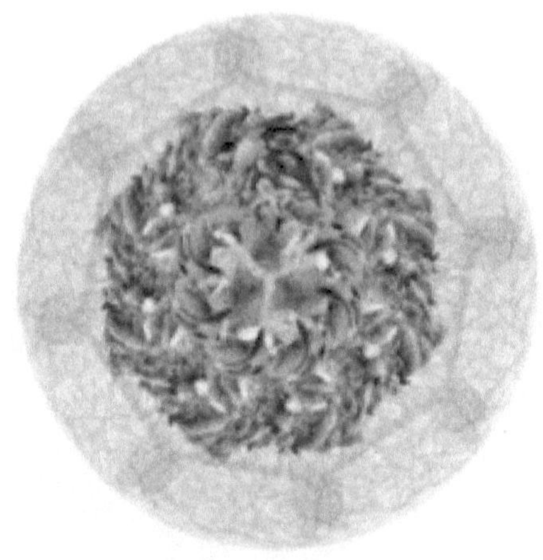

Plate. "Euro Tropiques" by Bernardaud, 2011. Fernando and Humberto Campana. http://www.maisonapart.com/edito/amenager-decorer/cuisine/les-campana-se-mettent-a-table-pour-bernardaud-p2-5140.php.

To some, the chair has come to represent a portrait of a country and an example of the essential Brazilian trait. Note the lack of specificity regarding which favela inspired the design of the chair. Favelization makes such details unnecessary; it allows for the treatment of all favelas and their realities as interchangeable. Specificity, a sign of attention, expertise and respect, is not required of the designers, those who sell the designs or the journalists who write about them.

While the Campanas + Lacoste project has not been the subject of extensive criticism, design critics such as those of the British publication *Creative Review* levied much criticism on the Favela Chair:

...the decadent nonsense that is the Favela chair.... Designed by current furniture design darlings, the

"Favela Mural," 2004. Fernando and Humberto Campana. Moss Gallery, New York City (closed in 2012). "The favela mural, created and built by Fernando and Humberto Campanas, is inspired, as was their favela chair, by the favela shantytowns of their native Brazil. This 20'x20' installation was built in December 2004, and will be a permanent part of the Gallery. Here are images of the mural in the context of the first three exhibitions at the Gallery." Moss Gallery website http://www.moss.coresense.com/gallery-exec/ display/campanas-wall.

Campanas, it must surely be one of the most fatuous products to come out of an industry increasingly in danger of disappearing up its own expensive upholstered behind. Its inspiration may have come from the slums of São Paulo, where desperate poverty forces inhabitants to make household objects out of whatever they can find, but the

> Favela is hand-built by professional craftsmen from virgin wood and sold by chi-chi Italian brand Edra for around £2000. Call it slum chic.[35]

Despite its lack of deeper exploration of why the reference to favelas renders it a "fatuous" design, *Creative Review* calls attention to the discrepancy between what the chair is supposed to represent and its materials, cost, and source. Regardless of terminology–slum chic, favela factor, or favelization–this critique is one of several to question what seems to be a larger trend in Brazilian design.[36] This type of favelization involves the creation of an image or object designed to "explain to the gringos, in a quick and vulgar manner, fin de siècle Brazil."[37] These images and objects provide foreigners a sense of recognition (because they reinforce certain stereotypes) while being innovative visually.

The Campanas have employed different types of favelization. And while their autobiography includes several mentions of favelas, but no information about direct connections between the designers and these communities. Another example of the favelization of a design came in the form of an offhand remark during an interview between the Campanas and Muniz in *Bomb* magazine. Fernando Campana said the following when describing their collaboration with Melissa, a shoe brand owned by the Brazilian company Grendene: "A larger percentage of recyclable materials will be used in the sandals, and the shoeboxes will have messages, like cigarettes [sic] packs here, about how and what to recycle. In Rocinha we'll have a drop box where people can put their old shoes so that the community can recycle them to

35. "Some Clever Ideas...," *Creative Review* (April 2007), 33.
36. Duarte, 2011.
37. Ibid.

make jewelry and other things."[38] There is no information on Grendene's, Melissa's, or the Campanas' website about any recycling initiative in Rocinha. In fact, a broader internet search failed to reveal information about the "drop box" referred to by Fernando Campana. Furthermore, Michele Levy, one of the owners of Melissa USA, stated she did not know whether such a recycling program was in place.[39] As the Campanas themselves state in their autobiography, the idea of the "recycling centers" (as they called them) was a suggestion they made to Grendene.[40] The fact that the suggestion was not put into practice by Grenene leads to a series of questions related to favelization: Why bring up the Rocinha in the context of the Melissa project? Fernando Campana's comment represents another example where a mere reference to favelas acts as an effective way of marketing otherwise purely commercial endeavors.

CAMPANAS + LACOSTE PROJECT

In 2006, Lacoste launched a Holiday Collector's Series, a yearly collaboration with designers to create a limited edition of polo shirts.[41] The Limited and Super Limited shirts were part of Lacoste's fourth Holiday Collector's Series, a collaboration with the Campanas entitled Campanas + Lacoste. The series featured six different shirts with arrangements of embroidered reptiles, a reference to both Lacoste's crocodile motif and the Campanas' Alligator Chair, a lounge chair upholstered

38. Vik Muniz, "Campana Brothers," Bomb Winter 2008, 14.

39. Email from Michele Levy, co-owner of Melissa USA, dated October 19, 2011.

40. Campana, 97.

41. "Campanas + LACOSTE," *Dezeen*, July 2, 2009, http://www.dezeen.com/2009/07/02/campanas-lacoste/.

with green stuffed alligators.[42] In 2005, Philippe Lacoste (grandson of Lacoste's founder) bought an Alligator Chair. Two years later, Lacoste approached the Campanas with a proposal for a potential collaboration. The designers created a project that reflects what they refer to as one of their "project attitudes," the "passage of one vocabulary that begins restricted to one production segment or one collection to another segment, in another scale, [made of] different materials."[43] In November 2012 a new set of Campanas + Lacoste shirts were issued. However, the focus of this chapter is solely the 2009 edition.[44]

The 2009 Campanas + Lacoste collaboration resulted in the creation of six types of shirts sold at different price points. The first set of shirts, named "Special Edition," were white short-sleeved polo shirts with a cluster of eight crocodiles in lieu of the label's signature single logo.[45] As noted by the *New York Times* blog, "[T]his understated and more wallet-friendly version…can be had for $165."[46] Twenty thousand Special Edition polo shirts were created, although information about their origin is unavailable and they were not made by Coopa-Roca. The huddle of alligators was supposed to show "how the reptiles pile up in mud beds during the dry season in their natural habitat."[47]

The second set of shirts designed by the Campanas for Lacoste were entitled "Limited Series." The mens' shirts had a cluster of anavilhanas, small fluvial islands found in

42. *Dezeen*, 2009.

43. Campana, 90.

44. Website of the Campanas + Lacoste collaboration, http://www.lacoste.com/campanas/.

45. Nytimes.com (blog), Nov. 4, 2009 and *Dezeen*, 2009.

46. Nytimes.com (blog), Nov. 4, 2009.

47. *Dezeen*, 2009.

the Amazon River, and the women's version had clusters of lianas, vines that grow in trees in tropical rainforests.[48] Coopa-Roca women hand-stitched 125 men's Limited Series shirts and the same amount of the women's using Lacoste logos of different sizes.

The "Super Limited Edition" shirts were the third set, and both men's and women's versions were made entirely from approximately 3,000 hand-stitched alligators.[49] The project's website indicated that only twelve Super Limited Edition shirts would be made to order. Buyers could choose to have the shirt made out of green, gold, or silver Lacoste logos.[50] *Wallpaper* magazine described this shirt as "Limited edition in the extreme," and noted it would be sold only through "key retailers such as London's Dover Street Market and Murray Moss in New York."[51] *The New York Times* noted, with a touch of humor, that the Super Limited Edition shirt "sells for–gulp–$7,000."[52]

The website for the Campanas + Lacoste project relied heavily on favelization in its description of the Limited and Super Limited shirts designed by the Campanas for Lacoste.[53] Information about where the Special Edition shirts (the cheapest ones with only eight alligators) were made is not available on the project's website. However, in regard to the other shirts, the website highlights:

48. "Competition: The Campana brothers for Lacoste," *Wallpaper* blog, September 15, 2009, http://www.wallpaper.com/fashion/competition-the-campana-brothers-for-lacoste/3686.

49. *Dezeen*, 2009.

50. Campanas + Lacoste project website, http://www.lacoste.com/campanas/#/the_concept.

51. *Wallpaper*, 2009.

52. NYtimes.com (blog), Nov. 4, 2009.

53. *Dezeen*, 2009.

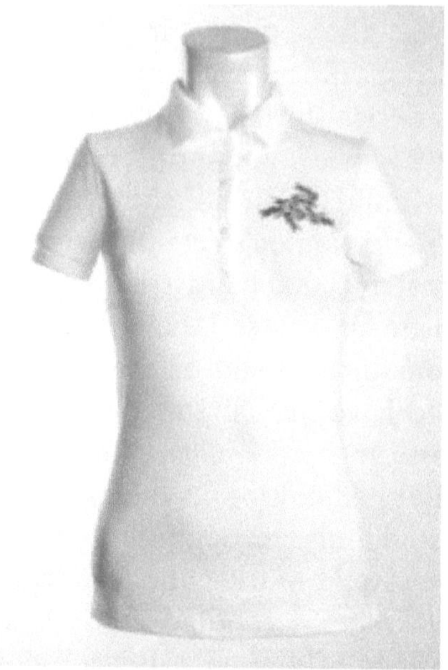

Shirt. "Women's Special Edition,"
2009. Fernando and Humberto
Campana. Courtesy of Lacoste.

The limited and super limited editions are produced
exclusively in cooperation with Coopa-Roca, a socially
responsible sustainable development organization based in
the Rocinha favela of Rio de Janeiro that provides work for
the very creative craftswomen and seamstresses who live in
that underprivileged neighborhood.[54]

This sentence merits closer analysis for many reasons.
First, it explicitly mentions the shirts were made in a
favela. The fact that the shirts were made by inhabitants
of a favela is not problematic. However, the text seems
to mention favelas in order to increase the attached value
of the shirts. Second, it employs an exaggerated number

54. Dezeen, 2009; Campanas + Lacoste project website; Wallpaper 2009.

Shirt. "Men's Special Edition," 2009.
Fernando and Humberto Campana.
Courtesy of Lacoste.

of descriptors to explain what Coopa-Roca is: (1) socially responsible, (2) sustainable, and (3) a development organization. Lastly, similar hyperbole is applied to the description of the people who made the shirts as: (1) women, (2) creative, (3) seamstresses, and (4) inhabitants of an underprivileged neighborhood. I recognize that descriptions of design as well as artwork, food, and travel are often accompanied by hyperbole. However, exaggeration can be misleading and, as in the case of the quote above, hyperbole might lend one to believe that a strictly commercial transaction (such as the purchase of a shirt) could accrue benefits to an underprivileged community beyond those reaped by the garment workers as a result of their contract with Lacoste. Lastly, while

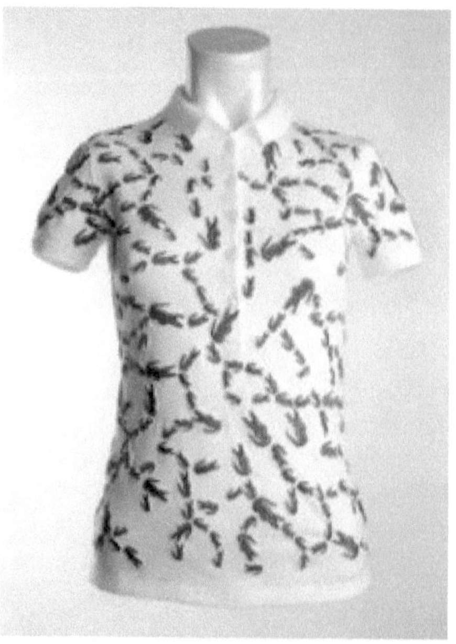

Shirt. "Women's Limited Edition,"
2009. Fernando and Humberto
Campana. Courtesy of Lacoste.

Rocinha is home to poor residents of Rio de Janeiro, its reality should not be oversimplified.

Numerous articles about Campanas + Lacoste echoed the language from the project's website. For example, *Interview* Magazine stated:

> For Lacoste's women's super limited edition (12 shirts will be produced) the Campanas turned the alligator logo into lace, inspired by Northern Brazil's lacemaking tradition, using 3000 of the little critters painstakingly hand sewn into a polo by seamstresses of the Coopa-Roca cooperative located in the Rocinha favela, Rio's largest slum with an estimated population of nearly 180,000 people... The shirt is truly tennis haute couture; each seamstress makes about

Shirt. "Men's Limited Edition," 2009.
Fernando and Humberto Campana. Courtesy
of Lacoste.

30 alligator's worth of lace per day, so one polo represents
100 days' labor.[55]

Like the project's website, the magazine *Interview* strongly
emphasized the fact that shirts were made by women
from a favela. However, it went further, highlighting the
intensity of the labor involved in making the shirts by
stating they were "painstakingly hand sewn" and that
"one polo represents 100 days' labor."[56] In sum, as argued
by Duarte, the project's website and related articles
turned the cooperative's human resources into public

55. Voight.
56. Ibid.

Shirt. "Women's Super Limited Edition," 2009.
Fernando and Humberto Campana. Courtesy
of Lacoste.

relations.[57] The socioeconomic reality and labor of the Coopa-Roca seamstresses was transformed into marketing for Lacoste's luxury products.

Consider the Q&A section of the Campanas + Lacoste website:

Question: Why did you choose the charity in Rio to work with?

Answer: We always wanted to give attention to the richness of Brazilian popular culture and the creativity of our country's handcrafts. By working with the community organization Coopa-Roca, we support serious projects and give the people [a] chance to increase their self-esteem.[58]

57. Duarte, 2010.

Shirt. "Men's Super Limited Edition," 2009.
Fernando   and   Humberto   Campana.
Courtesy of Lacoste.

This exchange is an example of favelization. First, Coopa-Roca is a cooperative, not a charity. Nevertheless, the unnamed interviewer addresses it dismissively as "the charity in Rio" as if there were only two relevant things about the organization: its (erroneous) categorization as a charity and its location in Rio. However, this mistake leads people to wonder whether, by buying these luxury items, they are somehow contributing to a charity. The Campanas + Lacoste project does not mention whether any percentage of its sales will be donated to Coopa-Roca. It would be reasonable to assume Coopa-Roca was hired by the project to stitch a certain number of shirts and

58. Campanas + Lacoste project website.

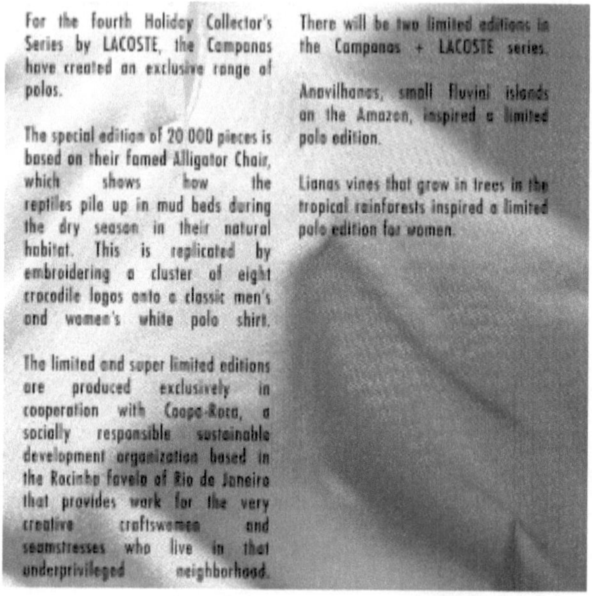

For the fourth Holiday Collector's Series by LACOSTE, the Campanas have created an exclusive range of polos.

The special edition of 20 000 pieces is based on their famed Alligator Chair, which shows how the reptiles pile up in mud beds during the dry season in their natural habitat. This is replicated by embroidering a cluster of eight crocodile logos onto a classic men's and women's white polo shirt.

The limited and super limited editions are produced exclusively in cooperation with Coopa-Roca, a socially responsible sustainable development organization based in the Rocinha favela of Rio de Janeiro that provides work for the very creative craftswomen and seamstresses who live in that underprivileged neighborhood.

There will be two limited editions in the Campanas + LACOSTE series.

Anavilhanas, small fluvial islands on the Amazon, inspired a limited polo edition.

Lianas vines that grow in trees in the tropical rainforests inspired a limited polo edition for women.

Campanas + Lacoste website. Screen shot captured on October 17, 2013, by the author. Courtesy of Lacoste.

get paid for its work just like it does with many other companies. The anonymous interviewer, by describing Coopa-Roca as a "charity," leads the unsuspecting reader to believe a potential purchase could benefit Coopa-Roca beyond the realm of the prices fixed and paid by the project.

On January 3, 2012, I interviewed the founder of Coopa-Roca, Maria Teresa Romeiro Leal (also known as TT or Tetê), to better understand her organization and the Campanas + Lacoste project. Her father was a physician and did volunteer work in Rio de Janeiro's favelas on Saturdays. Leal's mother was a teacher, and her oldest sister founded a school in 1960 that taught education

Campanas + Lacoste website. Screen shot captured on October 17, 2013, by the author. Courtesy of Lacoste.

and the arts to classes that included children of all backgrounds (upper- and middle-class as well as favela children). Leal attended classes at her sister's school between the ages of nine and seventeen, later teaching there on weekends. Leal received a degree in social science from the Federal University of Rio de Janeiro, where she says she sought out the Brazilian educator, Paulo Freire, and was greatly influenced by his teachings. At the time we first met, Leal resided in Leblon, one of the most expensive neighborhoods in Rio, and Coopa-Roca was her main professional activity.

During our meeting, Leal explained that in 1981, she went to the favela Rocinha for the first time with the housekeeper of a friend of hers. She then began going to the Rocinha every Saturday. During these trips she met this woman's neighbors and visited their homes. She noticed that they often decorated their homes using traditional handicraft techniques common in the northeast of Brazil. Leal said she realized their *"fazer"* (handicraft) was *"afetivo e cultural"* (imbued with affection and an example of cultural production). Her original intention was to create a non-governmental organization for children, but she eventually began working with women from Rocinha using leftover cloth from textile manufacturers. According to Leal, Coopa-Roca became known for extremely high-quality work and its attention to detail. According to the organizations website, they have done work for Osklen, M. Officer, Carlos Miele, Ernesto Neto, Interni, Fernando Jaeger, Paul Smith, Tord Boontje, Agent Provocateur, Ann Taylor, Cia. de Dança Deborah Colker, Citroen, and Christian Lacroix.

Leal stated another reason companies engage organizations like Coopa-Roca is *"responsabilidade social"* (social responsibility). She notes that, in relation to the Campanas + Lacoste project, the designers were "smart to unite the story of Coopa-Roca with the discussion of the Amazon," creating "a project that became Amazon + Rocinha + Lacoste + Campanas." Leal had approached the Campanas about potential collaborations on several occasions. When Lacoste approached the designers about Campanas + Lacoste, the designers wanted Coopa-Roca to make the shirts. Two contracts were signed: one between Coopa-Roca and the Campanas, another between Coopa-Roca and Lacoste. The agreements stated the number of shirts Coopa-Roca would sew, the date they would be delivered, and the fixed price to be paid per shirt. Coopa-Roca was originally supposed to make all the shirts for the project. However, Lacoste decided the cooperative would not make the Special Edition shirts sold for $125. Leal noted that this was a good decision because the cooperative, which sewed over 300,000 crocodiles logos over five months, would not have been able to produce more shirts. However, Leal stated that she does not know where the Special Edition shirts were manufactured even though the project's marketing gives the impression they were made by Coopa-Roca.[59]

Lacoste paid each Coopa-Roca seamstress US$1,000

for their work. Leal believed Lacoste paid well and thought the firm was easy to work with. However, she described certain issues related to the negotiations with the Campanas. According to Leal, the original contract the Campanas sent Coopa-Roca required the cooperative to pledge exclusivity: "that they would not sew again." Leal described negotiating with them over several weeks, explaining Coopa-Roca would agree never to sew logos for any other project, but could not grant the Campanas exclusivity in terms of sewing in general. She stated that the exclusivity clause was dropped from the final contract, but that negotiations on the matter were tense and put a strain on the relationship. I have been unable to secure copies of the original and final contract to evaluate what type of protection the Campanas wanted for their designs and how these protections, if agreed to by Coopa-Roca, would impact Coopa-Roca. However, what became clear from the interview is that all parties involved treated this project as business, that their relationship was contractual, and that payment for the shirts was pre-set. Campanas + Lacoste was not a charitable endeavor, nor were percentages of sales paid to Coopa-Roca. Perhaps most surprising was the discovery that Humberto, Fernando and Lacoste representatives never visited Coopa-Roca or Rocinha before the project started, during it, or after it ended. Does the fact that individuals who chose to actively highlight a cooperative from Rocinha in their marketing but did not visit the institution and surrounding community allow us to draw a certain type of conclusion?

---

59. Leal noted that the crocodile Lacoste logos came from Mexico and the white polo shirts were made in Peru.

REFERENCES TO FAVELAS

The oversimplification of the Other is a central characteristic of favelization. Another problematic aspect of the Q&A on the Campanas + Lacoste website is the casual reference to "the people" in the Campanas' answer. It creates a separation between an assumed "us" and "them." The individuals identified as "the people" are residents of Rocinha–not the potential consumers of the products being made, not members of Lacoste, or the designers themselves. "The people" are the "Other"–distant, different, yet somehow identifiable. Given that wealth is experienced in relative, not absolute, ways, this separation between "us" and "them" provides a certain degree of assurance that existing relations of power are being maintained.[60] Lastly, the Campanas say they are giving "the people" "a chance to increase their self-esteem."[61] Even if Coopa-Roca's initiatives do have an impact on the lives of the women it works with, this offhand reference trivializes the cooperative's endeavors and implies the Campanas and Lacoste believe favelados have low self-esteem.

Muniz and the Campanas are Brazilians who have, in their own way, employed some version of favelization in works that received considerable attention outside Brazil. The three men discuss this similarity in a conversation recorded in *Bomb* magazine:

> VM: How did your Favela project come about?
>
> HC: São Paulo is the largest recycling center in the world.
>
> FC: Other people's trash becomes useful for the poor

---

60. Robert H. Frank, *Luxury Fever: Weighing the Cost of Excess* (Princeton, NJ: Princeton University Press 2000),104.
61. Campanas + Lacoste project website.

people living on the streets. Cardboard boxes, wooden crates, they are all reused.

HC: This inspired us to make something out of nothing but what already exists. That was the idea: to create a world out of scarcity.

VM: When I am in Rio, I am extremely bothered by the "favela tours" in which khaki-clad tourists are driven around in safari-like jeeps so that they can take pictures of poor people.

HC: Your last exhibition in São Paulo, of photographs with classical themes made of piles of junk, makes me think of this recycling. Your vision for the show was so marvelous it made me jealous!

VM: Sometimes, through the use of materials, you are able to subvert ideas.[62]

This exchange is revealing in that it addresses the commodification of favelas by mentioning, for example, favela tours. However, Humberto Campana and Vik Muniz do not address the original question of how the Campanas' Favela Chair (described as the "Favela project") actually came about. The conversation continues with alarming superficiality and reduces the issue of favelas to something somehow synonymous with recycling and something artists can appropriate in different ways.[63] The interview reads like a conversation among people in search of beauty yet trying to recontextualize or justify their experimentation with "socially responsible" jargon. In fact, how Muniz and the Campanas talk about "the favela" reflects preconceptions and attitudes that merit further discussion.

The director of Coopa-Roca is aware of the cachet her organization provides for designers' projects. It could also be said that Coopa-Roca actively built its

62. Muniz,14.
63. Ibid.

international reputation through partnerships with well-known designers by using favelization.[64] The quality of their work may be extremely high, but the "favela factor" is also a reason why designers hire them. This dynamic may be something Leal is critical of today but it is an added value Coopa-Roca has promoted and defended, sometimes in its contracts. The contracts with the Campanas and Lacoste specified that Coopa-Roca's name would appear in connection with the project. However, neither contract specified *how* the organization would be described. Leal acknowledges this is something she thought about addressing only after she noticed situations where Coopa-Roca, its work, and its members were being mischaracterized. She acknowledges that while the cooperative did not make all the shirts for the Campanas + Lacoste project, the marketing and press coverage the project received made it seem as if they had.

However, as an example of what she considers egregious distortion, she cites an incident related to the designer Carlos Miele, not the Campanas + Lacoste project. Between 2001 and 2009, Coopa-Roca crocheted and embroidered clothing for M. Officer, Carlos Miele's Brazilian brand, and between 2002 and 2008, they worked on projects for the Carlos Miele brand. During our meeting, Leal described finding out that in a documentary for *Vogue TV* filmed in 2010, Miele spoke as if Coopa-Roca continued to work for his companies. Leal wrote *Vogue* and reached out to the journalist Suzy Menkes from the International Herald Tribune to protest this misrepresentation. She succeeded in removing the documentary from the internet. In January 2012, the documentary *The World of Carlos Miele* was still listed on

---

64. Coopa-Roca website, http://www.coopa-roca.org.br/
    projetos_especiaisI.asp.

YouTube, but the link was inactive.[65] I was able to secure a DVD copy of the video and it confirmed Leal's assertion that Miele refers to Coopa-Roca in a manner that would lead viewers to believe Coopa-Roca was still making clothes for the designer in 2010 In the *Vogue TV* video, Miele states:

> Ten years ago, I started a partnership with Coopa-Roca, which is a group of women living in a poor area of Rio de Janeiro. They do handmade craftsmanship with different traditional techniques from Brazil….With this partnership, we can keep the women at home, taking care of the kids and making a living. Fashion is a way of empowering women: women who wear my clothes and women that make my clothes. So fashion for me is a way of building a bridge between those two groups of women.

Miele describes his relationship with Coopa-Roca as a "partnership" even though the cooperative provided services as subcontractors. In her book *Design + Craft: The Brazilian Path*, Adélia Borges cautions against situations where those engaging in "social design" misconstrue their relationships with craftspeople. Miele's statement is an example of what Borges critiqued: a strictly commercial relationship is recast as a partnership so that the designer can describe the project in an altruistic (rather than contractual) manner.

Leal stated during our interview that she does not want "to create trouble but she does not want people to cross the line."[66] She stated bluntly that to say one works

---

65. I was able to obtain a DVD with a copy of the Vogue TV video from a public relations representative of Carlos Miele's New York store. However, the video contains no information as to the date it was issued. See Appendix 2 for a transcript of the video.

66. Maria Teresa Leal, interview by author, Rio de Janeiro, Brazil, January 3, 2012.

with Coopa-Roca and not contribute to it is *"sacanagem"* (unethical). She went on to say that such issues, and other factors, led her to alter Coopa-Roca's business strategy. Instead of sewing or embroidering clothing and objects for other entities, Coopa-Roca would now build its own brand. While Leal still wants to create a bridge between the nonprofit world and the private sector, she no longer wants to rely solely on partnerships with other companies/designers. "It's exhausting," she says about the latter, adding that she wants to make Coopa-Roca less dependent on them by developing the cooperative's own portfolio of products. Yet it is difficult to judge whether this new strategy will make Coopa-Roca, as an organization, more independent. During my visit to Coopa-Roca's store in Rio's Fashion Mall, I found the designs to be uninspired. In the store were the same lamps exhibited at the Cooper-Hewitt Museum's 2011 exhibit *Design With the Other 90%: Cities*–which were designed by Leal. These observations made me wonder: How do organizations that took advantage of favelization thrive without making use of it? What are the dynamics within Coopa-Roca that might contribute to a fuller understanding of favelization?

CONCLUSION

Despite the 2009 Campanas + Lacoste focus on favelas in its marketng, favelas were not invoked during the launch party held in Paris. The design and decoration of the event did not echo the focus placed on favelas in the marketing materials, highlighting instead another stereotype of Brazil, its tropical jungles. "During the Paris men's collections in June," noted *The New York Times*, "Fernando and Humberto escorted us through an elaborate jungle presentation staged inside a stunning

Parisian maison that featured their kooky crocodile creations."[67] The *maison* in question was the headquarters of the Ministry of Ecology, Energy and Durable Development, the opulent Hotel de Roquelaure on the Boulevard Saint Germain. The building was turned "into a mini Amazon, covering the hotel's parquet with a carpet of green grass and filling the rooms with a garden of tropical flowers and trees."[68] Not only was the theme of favelas absent from the Parisian launch party, the Campanas were described as the escort to foreigners venturing into the event. They were the evening's guides to Brazilianness.[69]

The images from the launch party in Paris differ significantly from the language used to advertise the Limited and Super Limited Edition shirts. For the party, the Campanas' nationality and the shirts' connections to Brazil were emphasized through decorations that alluded to the country's tropical image. No structures resembling shantytowns were erected, no semblance of the poverty of a favela could be found. Unlike the marketing materials for Campanas + Lacoste, the design of the Parisian party established no connection between the project and favelas. This dissonance reveals that luxury companies like Lacoste are selective about what version of Brazilianness they want to evoke when marketing a

67. NYtimes.com (blog), Nov. 4, 2009.

68. Voight.

69. Campana, 29. In their autobiography, Fernando states that he "likes it when an exhibit becomes a spectacle; I always wanted to be an actor, ever since I was a child I liked the theater and I never could practice acting per se, but set design yes." See also Yatzer, "Fernando and Humberto Campana for LACOSTE," (press release dated July 1, 2009), reprinted on the Yatzer website, http://yatzer.com/Fernando-and-Humberto-Campana-for-LACOSTE.

product: luscious tropical foliage for a party and favelas in its marketing.

Why did the Campanas + Lacoste project focus so much attention on the fact the products were made by women in a favela cooperative? Dark-skinned poor women, the demographic of Coopa-Roca, often face the greatest socioeconomic obstacles in Brazil. Discrimination in Brazil is class-, gender-, and race-based–or a mixture of all three. The creolization of cultures is part of the process of fetishization.[70] In the case of the Campanas + Lacoste advertisements, the women of a favela in Rio (arguably one of the most disenfranchised segments of Brazilian society) are used as a convenient Other. A luxury brand uses their reality to market luxury collectibles.

There is a difference between creating an object that reflects the reality of certain populations in Brazil and creating something that commodifies and fetishizes that same reality. The Campanas + Lacoste shirts and Favela Chair are luxury objects. The use of the word "favela" in the name or advertising of these designs begs the question: What image of Brazil were the Campanas trying to commodify?[71] The answer to this question lies in the

70. Okuwi Enwezor, "The Postcolonial Constellation: Contemporary Art in a State of Permanent Transition," *Research in African Literatures* 34 no. 4 (Winter 2003): 58.

71. Donna Paul, "Favela Forever," *Interior Design* Magazine (January 2005): 263. The Favela Chair led to commissions based on its design that were not related in any way to favelas. Murray Moss and Franklin Getchell commissioned the Campanas to construct a mural in the Moss Gallery reminiscent of the designers' Favela Chair. For their first permanent site-specific work in the United States, they "amplified a detail of the chair to create a kind of landscape," according to Fernando Campana. The panel is 22 feet long by 15 feet high and conceals a door to the back office. Murray Moss sees the installation as an "identifier for his gallery" which he considers "his theater." In fact, Moss compared the mural to "the rising of

fact that favelas might have originally represented an alternative to established stereotypes of Brazil, something genuine, raw, and in need of political attention.

What the Campanas do matters for many reasons. It matters because some believe that Brazil is "a country hardly bursting with design talent" and that "Mendes da Rocha aside, there has been little since Niemeyer's tropical modernism."[72] It matters because little is known about "Brazilian product and furniture design outside of the country apart from the Havaiana flip flops and the Campana brothers."[73] It also matters because, as the most famous Brazilian design team, what the Campanas do can further the stereotypes about what "Brazilian design" is, such as:

> Design in Brazil, the country of beaches and bikinis, soccer and the samba, has its own rhythm. The vibrancy of Rio's carnival, the pulse of the jungle, even the poverty of the people influenced the work of Brazilian architects and designers.[74]

The Campanas have almost become synonymous with the term "Brazilian design," so what they do matters. The Campanas are depicted as ambassadors of Brazilian design because media (Brazilian and foreign), international trade shows, museums, and publications want them to be so. "The Brazilianness of the Campana Brothers has been very good marketing indeed," noted one critic, and "they've been picked up by a western world with an almost embarrassing desperation for the exotic;

the chandeliers at the Metropolitan Opera"–a far cry from the reality of the favelas that inspired the shapes used in the mural.

72. Caroline Roux, "Interview: Campana Brothers," *Blueprint* 257 (2007): 54-57, as cited in Duarte, 2010.

73. Duarte, 2010.

74. Kelly Rude, "Discovering Brazil," *Canadian Interiors* 41 (2004): 30-35.

they have been embraced with more than just dull old enthusiasm."[75] Either by their own doing or the descriptions of others, many Campana products further the image of Brazil as "the other world," the antithesis of the Western world. As Bernard Rufosky wrote almost fifty years ago, "the exotic arts have long been appreciated in the Western world–not, however, without being cautiously dubbed primitive."[76] These should be words of caution to Brazilian designers and luxury companies or at least part of the analyses of how luxury brands and designers take advantage of a socially disadvantaged group to sell products. "For reasons which can certainly use close psychological inquiry," author Chinua Achebe once noted, "the West seems to suffer deep anxieties about the precariousness of its civilization and to have a need for constant reassurance by comparing it with Africa."[77] Brazil plays a similar role in the Western imagination; it becomes a place against which wealthier nations compare themselves, often with the mistaken belief that the wealth disparity in Brazil does not exist in their countries.

The issue for Brazilian designers therefore becomes: how to allude to aspects of Brazilian reality without fetishizing a country's social ills? Designers should seek partnerships with organizations such as Coopa-Roca to further efforts that create wealth in communities like Rocinha. However, if companies capitalize on the fact their products were made in a favela, they should describe these endeavors correctly and respectfully. If the

75. Roux, 54-57.

76. Lara 2009, 49, referencing Bernard Rudofsky, *Architecture Without Architects* (New York: Museum of Modern Art, 1964), 3.

77. Chinua Achebe, "An Image of Africa," (lecture, Chancellor's Lecture at the University of Massachusetts, Amherst, MA, February 18, 1975), 792.

intention is to market this aspect of a project, language should be agreed upon in conjunction with the favela-based organizations. There is, after all, a difference between cooperating with an organization located in a favela and using their reality as marketing. Given that many young Brazilian designers are establishing their professional presence overseas before being recognized in Brazil, how they promote themselves as Brazilians becomes particularly important. My hope is that they build successful careers without using a peoples' challenging existence, coupled with affluent customers' desire for exoticism, to motivate their products' sales.[78]

78. Muniz, 11.

FAVELIZATION IN DESIGN

When I first set off to investigate favelization, my objective was to focus on how this trend influenced the marketing of furniture. Specifically, I wanted to investigate how Brazilian designers born in the late 1970s and 1980s, with a strong understanding of the international luxury market, were using favelization to sell their products. A younger generation of designers seemed to be using the favelized vocabulary employed by previous generations like the Campanas and Carlos Miele in a way that suggested favelas were now firmly established as one of the stereotypes associated with Brazil. They were also attaching to it new themes such as violence and sustainability. In this chapter, I focus on three designs that are examples of favelization's growing popularity: the Neorustica furniture line by Brunno Jahara, and David Elia's Bala Perdida (Stray Bullet) chair and Pacificação (Pacification) shelves. While there are significant differences between Jahara and Elia, they are both Brazilian designers in their thirties who employ the tropes associated with favelas to brand high-end furniture as "Brazilian."

NEORUSTICA

The Neorustica furniture line was launched by Brunno

Jahara in 2010 and includes ten different pieces including cabinets, tables, a desk, and benches. According to the press release, each piece of "scrap wood" furniture is painted with nontoxic, water-based paint and is available in multicolored, "scratched white" or "scratched black" finish. A laminate made of recycled PET bottles lines the inside of certain Neorustica pieces. Jahara originally partnered with NDT Brazil, a furniture factory in Bady Bassitt, São Paulo, that "specializes in working with wood that is left over from construction sites or demolition." During our meeting in São Paulo, on January 12, 2012, he explained that NDT had since closed, and that negotiations were under way to shift the manufacture of Neorustica to a factory in the state of Parana.

During the interview, Jahara explained the creative process behind Neorustica. The design of the legs of each piece was inspired by the *banco caipira* ("country" or "hick" stool), a design Jahara considers universal. Jahara said he enjoys drawing inspiration from Brazilian themes or designs, yet at the same time he wants his designs to be understood throughout the world. He is passionate about improvisation, using unexpected materials, and "giving a soul" to objects. To make the Neorustica furniture decoration seem improvised, he assembled the colored slats randomly. In order to give them an aged patina, Jahara had the black and white pieces scratched after the paint dried. This technique reflects Jahara's belief that furniture should not have a "do not touch" design that stifles human interaction with it; it needs to be used, and should age well.

BALA PERDIDA (STRAY BULLET) CHAIRS

The Bala Perdida (Stray Bullet) chairs were designed in 2011 by David Elia, the owner of Studio Design da Gema.

Press release image of Brunno Jahara among examples of Neorustica furniture. Courtesy of Brunno Jahara.

"Babilonia Credenza," 2010. Brunno Jahara. Courtesy of Brunno Jahara.

Holes were made throughout each black or gray polypropylene plastic chair, and stainless steel eyelets were placed along the circumference of each hole. The

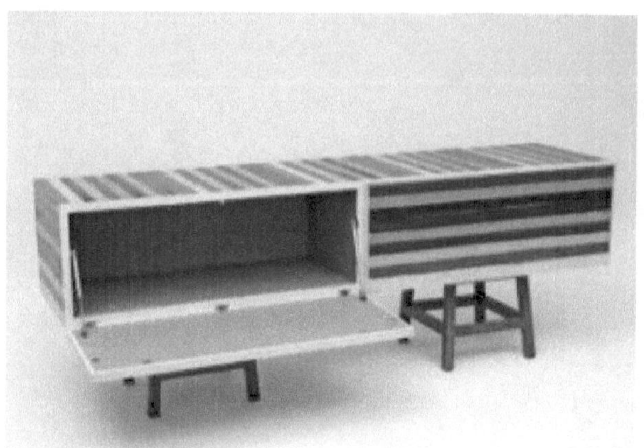

Inside of credenza made of PET bottle laminate, "Babilonia Credenza," 2010. Brunno Jahara. Courtesy of Brunno Jahara.

random placement of the holes made by Elia and his assistant is supposed to make the chair look as if it has been sprayed by bullets. The Stray Bullet chair is a limited edition collection consisting of eight black chairs priced at €6,000 plus one artist proof. Only one gray chair is available, for €15,000. There is also a 007 Moonraker Special Edition chair that, according to Design da Gema's website, was "inspired by the man with the golden gun and his visit to Rio during the 70's." Instead of stainless steel eyelets, this version of the chair has golden eyelets, and only two are available for sale for €12,000, plus an artist proof. In my email exchanges with Elia, he said that the Stray Bullet chairs were launched at the Hong Kong International Art Fair in 2012 at the booth of New York gallery L&M Arts.

PACIFICAÇÃO

The Pacificação (Pacification) collection consists of three

"Stray Bullet Chairs," 2010. Design de Gema. Courtesy of David Elia.

"Stray Bullet Chairs," 2010. Design de Gema. Courtesy of David Elia.

wooden shelves covered with miniature plastic toy houses from the board game Monopoly acquired in the United States and toy soldiers made in Italy. The entire

Details of the Stray Bullet Chair in black, 2010.
Design de Gema. Courtesy of David Elia.

piece is painted gold, and the top part of each shelf is
covered by a transparent glass top. Elia says he creates the
pieces himself, with the help of an assistant, in Monaco.
This is a limited edition of eight triptychs that sell for
€20,000 each. According to the Press Kit 2013, the
shelves represent "an assault in 3 dimensions, the choice
of the famous pieces gambling [sic] and toy soldiers,
painted in gold color symbolise both the plague of Rio?s
various traffics [sic] and the playful aspect, dear to the
heart of the Brazilian, who always manage to 'turn mud
into gold[.]'" In an email, Elia explained that he meant
that Brazilians are able "to do big things with very little."
In the same email, Elia stated that the gold paint is also
a reference to the exploration of gold that took place in
Brazil during colonial times. "Gold is very important in
Brazil's history of colonialism," wrote Elia. "Even in the
Brazilian flag the yellow color represents gold." In other
words, according to the designer, the piece is intended

to evoke contemporary themes (favelas, pacification campaigns, violence, and Brazilians' ability to improvise) as well as references to Brazil's colonial past. Nevertheless, the descriptions of Pacification in the press kit focus on the themes of violence, drug trafficking, and police intervention. They also repeat common stereotypes of Brazilians (that they are jovial, festive, and inventive despite adversity) by describing them as "playful" and "always" capable of turning something negative into something positive.

Shelves. "Pacification," 2012. Design de Gema. Courtesy of David Elia.

UNDERSTANDING THE INTERNATIONAL MARKET

Both Jahara and Elia understand the international luxury design market and how non-Brazilians perceive Brazil. They are middle- or upper-class Brazilians whose extensive transnational personal, educational, and professional experiences shape their design practices, branding, and business strategies. Jahara was born in Rio de Janeiro on January 9, 1979, and though Rio remained his hometown until he was 18, he spent a significant

Close-up of shelves. "Pacification," 2012. Design de Gema. Courtesy of David Elia.

amount of time outside of Brazil during his childhood. Jahara attended boarding school in England for a year, lived in India for six months, and traveled frequently abroad to such places as the United States, England, Germany, and Holland. Due to his Italian heritage, the designer secured a European passport and was able to live and work in Europe as a young adult. After high school, Jahara moved to Milan, and decided to study design. In 1997, he moved to Brasilia, Brazil's capital city (where his father lived at the time) to pursue an industrial design degree at the University of Brasilia. In 2001, he transferred to the Università IUAV di Venezia. During his time in Italy, Aldo Cibic (one of the members of the famed design group Memphis) became Jahara's mentor. The two designers had met in Brasilia during a design conference and grew closer during 2002 while Jahara was studying in Venice. During our interview, Jahara recalled with great affection the experience of house-sitting for Claudio Cibic (Aldo's brother) in an apartment full of Memphis furniture. In fact, Jahara's designs recall the

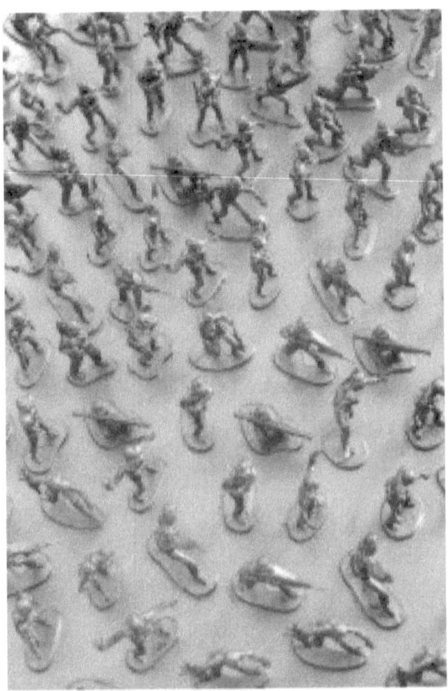

Toy soldiers. "Pacification," 2012.
Design de Gema. Courtesy of
David Elia.

playfulness of Memphis, and the use of color in
Neorustica is a strong example of how his connection
with Cibic may have influenced Jahara's work.

After one year in Venice, Jahara went to work at
Fabrica, a commercial research center in Treviso, Italy,
owned by Benetton. Jahara was one of fifty people from
around the world chosen for a design apprenticeship.
From 2002 to 2004, he worked closely with Jaime Hayón,
a designer from Spain and head of Fabrica's design
department. "During my stay at the Communication
Research Center," writes Jahara on his LinkedIn profile,
"we developed a series of products for Fabrica Features,
art directed editorial projects, and created interior design
for exhibitions and a number of clients internationally."

Jahara regards his training at Fabrica as a formative experience.

Jahara says he returned to Venice in 2004 with a scholarship and a studio sponsored by the Fondazione Bevilacqua La Masa. He was the first designer sponsored by the foundation (which usually supports only contemporary artists) and used his two-year stay in Venice (2004-2006) to experiment with different materials. Between 2006 and 2008, Jahara lived and worked in Venice and Amsterdam. From May 2008 to August 2008, he worked in Milan as a graphic consultant to the director of *Domus* magazine, Flavio Albanese. Jahara's years in Italy brought him in contact with major figures from the design world and exposed him to the dynamics of the international design market.

In 2009 Jahara returned to Brazil. As the economic situation in Europe worsened in 2008 and 2009, he had contemplated moving either to Tokyo or to São Paulo. The fact that Brazil's economy was doing well persuaded him to choose the latter. When we met, he had two assistants working with him in his studio. In my interview, Jahara noted that despite the difficulty of working as a designer in Brazil (high costs, unreliable suppliers, and limited options of what can be manufactured industrially), he finds that hard work is valued, and enjoys that most Brazilian furniture manufacturers still approach production as a craft. According to his website, Jahara has exhibited his work at many international venues, such as La Bienniale di Venezia (Art and Architecture), and high-profile museums like the Centre Georges Pompidou in Paris.

David Elia was born on April 10, 1982, in Rio de Janeiro. His father is originally from Lebanon, his mother from Uruguay. Design da Gema's press kit describes Elia as someone who "grew up between France, the United States and Brazil, making him not only a true Brazilian but also a citizen of the world." Between 1985 and 1990, Elia attended the Lycée Français Molière in Rio. When his family moved to the Principality of Monaco in 1996, he enrolled in the Lycée Albert 1er, where he pursued a French baccalauréat. Elia said he returned to Rio once or twice every year during this time to visit friends and family. For his bachelor's degree in fine arts, Elia attended Brandeis University in Waltham, Massachusetts, between 2000 and 2004. In 2002 he obtained a certificate in architecture from Harvard University's graduate school of design. Elia has two masters degrees: one in interior architecture from the Rhode Island School of Design in Providence (2004-2007) and another in industrial design from Domus Academy in Milan, Italy (2008-2009).

Elia's professional experience is as international as his educational background. He interned at Moshe Safdie and Associates in Cambridge, Massachusetts (2006), then worked as a junior designer at Djandji Interior Design in Monaco (2007) and Arteplan Achitecture & Interiors in Paris (2008). In 2010 he worked at the Estudio Campana in São Paulo as a junior design, where he helped create prototypes using the new materials the Campanas brought to the studio. Elia received the German International Forum Materials Design Award for the project Capella Acoustic Tile in 2010, and in 2011 he received the Italian A' Design Award in Arts, Crafts and Ready-Made Design for the tray "Reel," made of corrugated cardboard with a latex water-based coat and a glass top. This tray was sold at the MoMA Store in 2012 for $50.

Elia founded Design da Gema in Rio de Janeiro in early 2010 once his work at the Estudio Campana came to an end. He says he chose Rio because it is the Brazilian city that inspires him the most and the city he is most familiar with. Two years later he decided to move back to Monaco. Over email Elia explained that he decided to leave Rio because he felt his daily routine in the city was becoming dangerous. He frequently had to go to "industrial zones of Rio for meeting[s] with artisans and it was during much pacification and interventions of the police in the Favelas." Elia said he was not scared of staying in Rio, but his family "strongly encouraged [him] to leave and relocate the studio somewhere else." Elia feels that leaving Brazil is not an obstacle and believes that globalization and the internet make it easier for Brazilian artists to live and work outside Brazil. In an email he cited Vik Muniz as an example (Muniz lived for many years in Brooklyn before returning to Brazil). Elia feels it "is not necessary to be full time in Rio but [he] can still go there temporarily for getting inspiration." Design da Gema's press kit states there are showrooms in both Rio de Janeiro and Monaco. Elia said he keeps a few examples of his work in Rio and maintains a commercial space for meetings. The Press Kit 2013 lists François Pinault as the owner of a Stray Bullet chair (as well as three other designs by Elia) and Paula Cusi de Azcarraga and Prince Albert II of Monaco as owners of his Desmatamento (Deforestation) chair.

Despite the fact that Elia lives in Monaco, Design da Gema's website reads as if its main operations were still based in Brazil. The landing page states that "Design da Gema is a combination of a design studio and a small production unit born and raised in Rio de Janeiro, Brazil. Through the union of design and art, products are made with a touch of poetry inspired by Carioca urban life." This quote, as well as the studio's entire branding, focuses on a connection between Rio de Janeiro and the designer ("Carioca" is the term used to describe something or someone from Rio). Elia noted he wanted the website to be playful, urban, beautiful, and colorful, as well as focused on Rio de Janeiro's main attractions. He commissioned two Cariocas to create the site's illustrations, the street artist Mateu Velasco and the graphic designer Aline Horta, who graduated from Central St. Martins in London. Colorful drawings show stylized favelas among the statue of Christ the Redeemer, Sugar Loaf, and Maracanã stadium.

In short, as their biographies reveal, Jahara and Elia have extensive international experience and a strong awareness of the international design market, contemporary trends in Europe and the United States, and how Brazil is perceived outside the country.

PRESS MATERIALS PREPARED BY THE DESIGNERS

The media, and blogs in particular, play an important role in the favelization of furniture. Most posts published in Brazil and abroad copy language from the press releases, contributing further to the favelization of the collection. During our interview, Jahara stated that journalists writing about his work simply cut and paste (with slight modifications) the text from his press releases. They usually ask him for a press package (which contains a press release and photographs), but few request an interview, he said. Elia made a similar observation. He said that most bloggers do not reach out to him for information and, instead, copy language and images from other blogs. Jahara echoed Elia's comment stating that, because of the internet, communication has become "viral, one site copies another." In other words, Jahara and Elia are aware that if they create a powerful narrative, journalists, in a rush to generate new content, rarely challenge the press pitch they receive. Jahara told me he writes his own press releases, and his sister, who lives in London, translates these into English. It is reasonable, therefore, to consider the language in the Neorustica press release an example of the designer's own marketing strategy, and not one created for him by an external marketing agency. Jahara is not only responsible for crafting the presentation of his designs, he is also keenly aware of how the press release language determines how journalists will describe his work.

The press materials for all three collections employ favelization. In the press release titled "Neorustica Furniture Collection" emailed to me by Jahara on September 7, 2011, Jahara states that each piece in the collection is named after a favela in Rio de Janeiro, such as Vidigal, Rocinha, Dona Marta, Tuiuti, Caricó, Vila Canoa, Uribu, and Pavão. The text of Neorustica's press release takes the collection's association with favelas several steps further. It states that the furniture "pays homage to the country's rural background and has the contrasts of [B]razilian culture." By explicitly ascribing to the furniture the role of "homage," the press release attempts to recast the utilitarian objects as a tribute to favelas. Jahara's text describes the designer as someone who "wants to highlight the living condition of people that moved from the countryside into big cities searching for a better life (i.e., improvised homes made of scrap)." The press release identifies Rio de Janeiro as Jahara's hometown.

Like Fernando Meirelles and Vik Muniz, Jahara has experience in advertising. At Fabrica's Communication Research Center, creative professionals work with different forms of media, ranging from design, music and

"Vidigal Side Table/Bed Side Table," 2010. Brunno
Jahara. Courtesy of Brunno Jahara.

"Dona Marta Low Table," 2010. Brunno Jahara.
Courtesy of Brunno Jahara.

film to photography, publishing, and the Internet. It is
likely that, as the website for Fabrica puts it, Jahara

"Carico Single Drawer," 2010. Brunno Jahara.
Courtesy of Brunno Jahara.

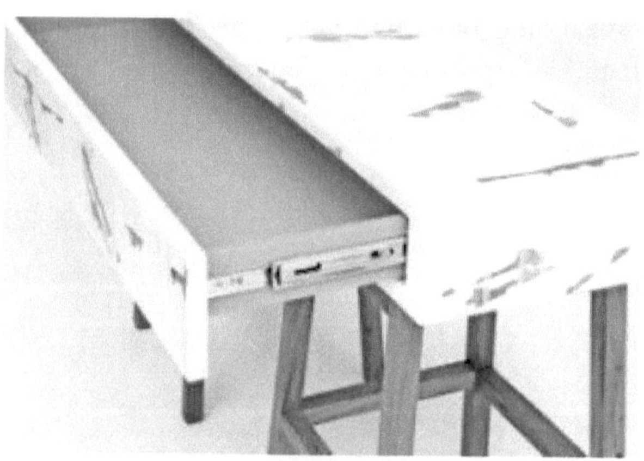

Interior of Drawer, "Carico Single Drawer," 2010.
Brunno Jahara. Courtesy of Brunno Jahara.

experimented with "blurring the boundaries of culture
and language and transgressing the traditional borders
between a diverse range of communication mediums."
In 2010, Jahara worked as an art director at DM9DDB,
one of Brazil's largest and most prominent advertising

"Dona Marta Low Table," 2010. Brunno Jahara.
Courtesy of Brunno Jahara.

agencies. As part of DM9DDB's Innovation Department, the designer focused on advertising connected with industrial design and the fashion industry. Jahara undoubtedly brings to his current design practice (and the marketing of his own products) the sales expertise honed at Fabrica and DM9DDB.

Unlike Jahara, who created an individual press release for each of his projects, Design da Gema circulates a press kit that is several pages long and contains information about all the studio's projects, as well as sections about the designer, his inspirations, and Rio de Janeiro's violence. While Jahara drafts his own marketing material, in 2012 Elia hired Marina Péré, the director of the French communications company Heaven Nice Com, to draft the press kit in French and later had it translated in France into Portuguese and English. The Press Kit 2013 describes the Stray Bullet chair as: "Survivor of daily fights that plague the northern districts of Rio, the chairs of the collection Stray Bullet represent the essence of the artist's work of turning a chronicle of ordinary urban violence into artwork." This description personifies the chair as a "survivor" of Rio's violence. It also states that violence is the studio's "manifesto" and describes the Stray Bullet collection as "open[ing] a window into this world as well as one's conscience." One infers that the "world" mentioned in the press kit is the violence of Rio de Janeiro. The text goes on to describe the chair as the "beginning" of how Elia's designs will approach the violence. It is interesting to note that the press kit states that "violence was never really explored in design" despite the fact that numerous postmodern and conceptual designers (including Brazilian designers) have addressed violence in their work. (Marcio Kogan, Isay Weinfeld, Vlieger & Vandam, Studio Oooms, and Philippe Starck are some examples.) This erroneous statement does, however, support Elia's use of violence as a signifier of novelty, differentiation, daring, and attached value.

The absence of the word "favela" in Design da Gema's web and press kit descriptions of the Stray Bullet collection does not mean they are not examples of favelization. There is a high concentration of favelas in the northern region of Rio, and stray bullets in Rio are often the result of the exchange of fire in favelas. The Chilean blog *Joia Magazine* addressed these connections in its description of the chair, stating it "looks like it had been the target of a gunfight in some part of the favela."[1] Furthermore, as noted in the chapter "Favelization in Film," in the context of the movie *City of God*, violence is one of the tropes of favelization. While this theme is most evident in film, the description of the Stray Bullet chair is an example as well. Interestingly, Elia shared with me a document titled "Selected Bibliography Supporting

---

1. Joia Staff, "Stray Bullet, la silla tiro al blanco," *Joia Magazine*, August 9, 2011, http://www.joiamagazine.com/tag/stray-bullet.

Design da Gema Research," which lists nine sources. Fifth on the list is Paulo Lins's book *City of God* (1997). In an email, as additional sources of inspiration for his work, he listed movies *Tropa de Elite, City of God, Black Orpheus,* and *Moonraker* from the James Bond series. The blog *Lost in a Supermarket* drew a connection between the Stray Bullet chair and the well-known film *City of God*, stating the chairs are "customized to look like they (barely) survived a day in the life of City of God."[2]

Like Jahara, Elia uses language in his press materials to ascribe his objects a symbolic role. Design da Gema's press kit states the Stray Bullet chair is an example of "how a work of art can convey awareness to the eye of the observer." This language describes the chair as capable of informing viewers (of all backgrounds and nationalities) about the violence in Rio de Janeiro. *Icon Magazine* repeated this portrayal, describing the chairs as "inspired by the violence present in Carioca life, bringing awareness to this critical subject matter."[3] The attempt to imbue the chairs with symbolic political meaning is an example of how the designer politicizes a luxury object as a way of creating attached value.

The favelization of the Pacification shelves is explicit: Elia's press kit links the Pacification shelves directly to favelas. The name "pacification" is a translation of "pacificação," a term used to describe the Força de Pacificação (Pacification Force) campaigns carried out by the Brazilian army and military police in Rio de Janeiro's

---

2. "Buy a Chair Riddled with Brazilian Stray Bullets… On Purpose," Lost in a Supermarket, August 12, 2011, 2012, http://lostinasupermarket.com/2011/08/buy-a-chair-riddled-with-stray-bullets-on-purpose/.

3. "Design da Gema," *ICON* Magazine, November 2011, Issue 101, accessed on Design da Gema's website on August 23, 2013, http://www.designdagema.com/.

favelas since the end of 2008. The press kit goes on to state:

> "All is serious, nothing is serious" could summarize the collection "Pacification," inspired by the raids of the army, police and special police (BOPE) in the favelas, which causes as many deaths as they save lives in the perpetual fight against gangs which "hold" neighborhoods.

This description links the three gold-painted shelves and the often violent, ongoing actions by the army and police in Rio de Janeiro favelas. It also expresses the opinion that these actions cause as many deaths as they save. Furthermore, it begins with a quotation that is supposed to "summarize the collection." In reality, this quotation has the effect of diminishing the political import of the subject of the shelves (pacification). It turns the notion of pacification into something not serious, voyeuristic, and carnivalesque.

Screen shot. Design da Gema's Instagram showing the prototype of a table that is part of the Stray Bullet collection, captured on October 29, 2013, by the author.

Screen shot. Design da Gema's Instagram showing the prototype of a table that is part of the Stray Bullet collection, captured on October 29, 2013, by the author.

THE MEDIA'S ROLE IN FURTHERING FAVELIZATION

During my research, I reviewed twenty-one articles, websites, and blog-posts about Neorustica dated, published, or available online between October 2010 and December 2011. I was curious to see how many repeated the press release's references to favelas. Twelve out of the twenty-one sources mentioned favelas in their coverage of Jahara's furniture. Seven articles did not contain any mention of favelas: one in Spanish, three in English, and another three in Portuguese. I was unable to translate the content of blog posts written in Danish and Chinese. Most editorials used terms from the press release such as "favela," "shanty towns," and "homage." For example, Designboom noted each piece in Jahara's collection "is named after a shanty town or favela in [R]io de [J]aneiro."[4] The website Because London adapts the

4. "Designbloom," Jahara Studio, November 23, 2010,
   http://www.brunnojahara.com/presspages/press_jahara_designboom.html.

language of the press release somewhat, describing the furniture as a "commentary on rural Brazilian living," and stating:

> ...Jahara wants the range to highlight the living conditions of those in the favelas–people who have moved from country to city in search of a better life, and whose resourcefulness in times of need never fails to astonish...the names of the pieces... are homage to shanty towns or favelas in Rio de Janeiro.[5]

Again, the influence of the press release is obvious. What became evident after reading the news coverage of Neorustica is that many journalists took language directly from Jahara's press release. In doing so, they, as well as their publishers, further globalized the language and imagery of favelization.

The article entitled "Wastemaker," published in the April 2011 edition of *Wallpaper* magazine, is an example of how closely the language in articles about Neorustica mirrors that of the press release and how favelization spreads through different media, in different countries. The article includes a colorful picture of the Babilonia credenza and two paragraphs of text.[6] Like the press release, *Wallpaper* describes the furniture not as something of value because of its design and craftsmanship, but from the attached value that inheres in the designer's background and in the supposed connection between the Neorustica furniture line and Rio de Janeiro's favelas. *Wallpaper* does not challenge the stereotypes used in the Neorustica press release, and by

---

5. "Because London," Jahara Studio, November 24, 2010,
   http://www.brunnojahara.com/presspages/press_jahara_becauselondon.html
6. "Planeta Casa: Ideas e produtos para um mundo sustentável," Casa *Claudia* 4 (April 2011), 52.

repeating its language, propagates the favelization of the furniture collection.

The repetition by blogs of language provided by the designers was perhaps even more obvious in the case of Design da Gema. During my research, I reviewed sixteen articles, websites, and blog posts about the Stray Bullet chair dated, published, or available online in August to November 2011. As of August 16, 2013, the Pacification shelves had not received any press coverage. On his website, Elia used language personifying the chairs as survivors of a shooting. Over email he explained that he made up the story about rescuing a chair "to make it more fun even though there are serious undertones." According to the designer, it is a "playful way of saying how the inspiration came from the shootings occur[r]ing in the fave[l]as during pacification and police raids everyday." Even though he removed this narrative from the website in 2012 ("replacing it with just a straightforward explanation just in case people did not catch the irony"), most of the press coverage of the chair repeats versions of this story. *DesignMilk*, for example, wrote in 2011 that the "Stray Bullet Chair was inspired by a real chair that was stuck in a bar shooting." *Complex* reiterated Elia's personification with even greater flourish the same year:

> Design da Gema turns tragedy into seating with tremendous narrative quality through the Stray Bullet Chair. After a shooting at a carioca bar in the Northern Zone of Rio de Janeiro, an injured chair was relocated to the firm's office. Heralded as a survivor, Design da Gema has made the bullet riddled chair into a luxury item.

Complex attempts to explain the creation of a luxury item tied to the theme of violence and asserts it has "tremendous narrative quality." The version of favelization employed by Elia draws on a brand of exoticism attached to the violence of Rio de Janeiro, a trope that has been disseminated globally.

FAVELAS AND FAVELADOS: THE USEFUL OTHER

Throughout history, national, religious, socioeconomic, and ethnic groups identified certain peoples as the Other. The creation of an Other often facilitated a definition of oneself; it also facilitated the creation or preservation of hierarchies. In *The Death of Authentic Primitive Art: And Other Tales of Progress*, Shelly Errington described how the Other developed in Europe during the nineteenth century. "As Europeans increasingly came to think of themselves during the nineteenth century as essentially and characteristically secular, rational, civilized, and technologically advanced," Errington states, "they almost necessarily generated an imagined Other that was savage, ignorant, and uncivilized."[7] As discussed in the Introduction, to many Brazilians from the formal city, favelados are the Other. Favelization introduces the favela as an Other to the rest of the world.

The Neorustica press release and the articles about Jahara's collection rely on stereotypes about poverty in Brazil and about favelas in particular. Favelados become a marginalized Other whose presence buttresses the identity of the wealthy consumer. Favelas also come to represent a manufactured source of attached value. This type of favelization is similar to how American advertisers used references to native peoples in the nineteenth century. In "Reduced to Images: American Indians in Nineteenth-Century Advertising," Jeffrey

---

7. Shelly Errington, *The Death of Authentic Primitive Art: And Other Tales of Progress* (Berkeley: University of California Press, 1998), 16.

Steele argues that nineteenth-century American advertising relied on a "rich and complex carnivalesque tradition" of using various racial and ethnic minorities to create a "sense of white, middle-class consumer solidarity at the expense of subordinate groups."[8] American Indians were used as signifiers of nature, the primitive, and danger in advertising materials for a broad range of products in the United States during the 1800s. According to Steele, Indians were an emblem of racial otherness that advertisers "reduced to images that could be made to play allotted roles in nineteenth-century fantasies of cultural imperialism."[9] As Steele notes simply: "Stereotypes sell."[10] Jahara and Elia are examples of designers who use stereotypes connected to favelas to sell luxury objects. Unlike the American Indian in nineteenth century advertising, favelados do not signify nature, but they have come to represent danger, the primitive, and to a certain extent, the "unknown" realms of otherwise knowable cities.

Favelas and favelados represent the Other not only to non-Brazilians, but to Brazilians as well. Even though the *Wallpaper* article states that the Neorustica furniture line was designed to highlight the living conditions of Brazilians who live in the country's favelas, most middle- and upper-class Brazilians will never set foot in a favela in their lifetimes. Interactions among social classes in Brazil occur frequently, but in structured, hierarchical relationships (e.g., master and servant) and outside favelas. Rio de Janeiro's slums, in particular, are regarded

8. Jeffrey Steele, "Reduced to Images: American Indians in Nineteenth-Century Advertising," *The Gender and Consumer Culture Reader* (New York: New York University Press, 2000), 110, 112.

9. Ibid., 123.

10. Ibid., 109.

by many residents of the formal city as lawless enclaves controlled by gangsters, militias, and corrupt police. The otherness of favelados is a reality of Brazilian society. Some designers, like Jahara, reference this stratum of Brazilian society in their marketing materials selectively, emphasizing the poverty and hardships of the favelados while downplaying the stereotypes of violence and crime. Elia, on the other hand, focuses on the violence generated in favelas and its impact on the formal city. In both types of marketing, favelas and their inhabitants are used as a point of contrast–a space and population that is different from the target consumer for the luxury products being advertised.

Favelization is, to borrow Steele's terminology, a rich and complex carnivalesque trend. The word "carnivalesque" is used to describe something suggestive of a carnival, or marked by an often mocking or satirical challenge to authority and the traditional social hierarchy. Favelization is also an example of the relationship between notions of the carnivalesque and primitivist discourse. In the book *Gone Primitive: Savage Intellects, Modern Lives*, Mariana Torgovnick argues that the essence of the carnivalesque is that "one cannot tell male from female, rich from poor, black from white: those differences, ordinarily so crucial, do not matter for the duration of the carnival."[11] The carnival represents a time, she continues, that is freer, filled with the illusion that "everything is possible."[12] But, she cautions that "the interpenetration of third and first world is not just festive. Behind the festivities are social and economic facts we should not forget."[13] This is precisely the

11. Torgovnick, 40.
12. Ibid.
13. Ibid.

problem that lies behind the "festive" reference to favelas in marketing materials for luxury goods. The use of carnivalesque notions of the Other "ignores the real social and economic cost of the global village"; as Torgovnick notes accurately, a critique of these notions "might sound a discordant note at the carnival," but it is morally imperative to sound that note "in the ghettoes and shantytowns of the urban jungle, especially in third world cultures."[14] Design da Gema's website and marketing language are both suggestive of a carnival and marked by a satirical challenge to gravity of the violence that takes place in Rio de Janeiro. The webpage that shows the Stray Bullet chair includes images of Rio's Carnival. Stylized animations of people in costumes (and favelas) appear alongside photographs of the chair. The website is a visual example of Elia's conflation of the carnivalesque and violence, and the press kit emphasizes it:

> Behind the picture of Rio de Janeiro, its pristine sandy beaches, its carnival or the Corcovado, lies a very different reality, where the favelas are the scene of daily violence and insecurity between cartels and military police. But the Cariocas, as they often do for everything that is related to art, recover violence and anger turning them into creative energy. Here more than anywhere, life is stronger than death. This state of urgency encourages them to enjoy every moment, generates vivid colors, breathtaking music rhythms, and beautiful dances. This idea can be best illustrated by the world renowned carnival of Rio.

This language creates a direct connection between the violence of Rio and the colors, music, and dancing associated with Carnival. Furthermore, the language of the website parodies the impact of violence by saying that

---

14. Torgovnick, 41.

the residents of Rio "recover violence and anger turning them into creative energy" and that the "state of urgency" experienced in the city actually acts as a catalyst for cultural expressions "best illustrated by" Carnival.

Another example of Design da Gema's carnivalesque marketing language is found in the 2013 press kit description of the Pacification shelves. The text states that the quotation "All is serious, nothing is serious" summarizes the Pacification shelves. Does it mock the reality of pacification? In our email communications, Elia noted that there is much to say about Design da Gema's "playful aspects [and] the more serious undertones and a more in[-]depth analysis of all the stratas of social life in Brazil that" the designer tries to reinterpret in his work. He states that works like the Pacification shelves and Stray Bullet chairs are capable of "bringing into reality and consciousness the violence and security present in Brazilian society and especially Rio." Using a similar tone, the press kit notes that in Rio, "life and death constantly collide side by side, without compromising the vividness of the place." Once again, the gravity of themes like violence are dismissed with a mocking generalization.

IMPROVISATION, IMPERMANENCE, AND PRIMITIVISM

The focus on the impermanence and improvisation of favela construction furthers the image of favelados as primitive. The notion that favela homes are made out of wood, in an improvised manner, and are inherently precarious becomes especially relevant in the context of favelization, since many of the examples of this trend employ these stereotypes. For example, the interior designs of the restaurant Favela Chic in Paris and London create a visual representation of favelas by creating an environment that relies heavily on exposed plywood.

Impermanence is a signifier of primitivism, as noted by David Brody in *Visualizing American Empire: Orientalism and Imperialism in the Philippines*. "Western culture in general understood the hut's impermanence as uncivilized and culturally unstable," argues Brody, "connoting the world of the primitive through its inhabitants' adherence to a type of ephemeral building."[15] A reference to the type of housing of a group of people is used as a way of identifying how they are different (and less civilized). What might read at first like an aesthetic evaluation is more problematic; it is a moral judgment placed on impermanence.

In *Gone Primitive*, Torgovnick describes Western tropes of primitivism. Primitives are compared to children and therefore "intuitive, spontaneous, and irrational."[16] In order to emerge into modernity, "the cultural equivalent of adulthood," primitives need guidance from individuals or groups outside their communities. Despite their need for guidance, she states "that primitives [are] incapable of responding to the gentle guidance of the West, and requir[e] severe control."[17] According to Torgonick, whites were destined or obliged to control and dominate primitive peoples and their territories.[18] Favelization involves the selective application of familiar Western tropes about the primitive to the descriptions of favelados. In the chapter on film, I discussed the themes of guidance and transcendence in the context of Vik Muniz's documentary *Waste Land*. I would argue that descriptions

---

15. David Brody, *Visualizing American Empire: Orientalism and Imperialism in the Philippines* (Chicago: University of Chicago Press, 2010), 13.
16. Torgovnick, 99.
17. Ibid.
18. Ibid.

that portray favela housing as "improvised" actually suggest a need for guidance; they imply that favelados are in need of help from outsiders in order to build proper homes.

The Neorustica press release echoes the stereotypes associated with favela housing when it states that the Neorustica furniture is "built with a feel of improvisation" similar to that of homes in a favela. The text dismissively describes favela dwellings as "improvised homes made of scrap." Furthering the perceived connection between Neorustica's roughly hewn finish and real favelas, the press release also states that the wood used to make the pieces is "left over from construction sites or demolition."

The press package for the Campanas' Favela Chair, produced by Edra, which preceded Neorustica by seven years, makes similar use of these stereotypes. In December 2011, I received from the Estudio Campana's press relations officer the marketing materials related to the Favela Chair. In the body of the email was a brief description in Portuguese stating, "Originally, it was made of pieces of wood from crates used to carry fruit that is sold at markets. The idea was the result of observations of the accumulation of materials in favelas. Fernando and Humberto tried to imitate the intuitive construction of houses in favelas."[19] As noted earlier, Torgovnick argues the word "intuitive" is often used to describe the primitive. In the bilingual press release

19. Julia Tereno, email to author, December 16, 2011. The original text in Portuguese read: "Poltrona Favela (2003)/Dimensões: 67 x 74 x 62 cm/ Material: Madeira/Produzida pela Edra, na Itália/Originalmente, foi feita de tiras de madeira tiradas de caixas de frutas usadas em feira. A ideia veio a partir da observação do acúmulo de materiais em favelas. Fernando e Humberto tentaram imitar a maneira intuitiva de construção das casas em favelas."

attached to the email, the descriptions of the chair in English and Italian are more dramatic. The one-page document contains two images: a picture of the Favela Chair in front of an all-white background and another of the chair positioned in the corner of a baroque-style interior, with ornate plaster and wood moldings, a large gilt candelabra, and patterned floor tiles. There are two clusters of text. The larger text box, placed on a white background, describes the Favela Chair as "small pieces of recycled wood put together by hand [that] become a primitive throne of symbolic elegance."[20]

The Favela Chair press release does not contain additional language explaining the words "primitive" and "symbolic." As a result, the English- or Italian-speaking reader is left to interpret this nod to primitivism and symbolism only within the context of the reference to favela in the smaller text box. The text is a smaller font superimposed onto the picture of the Favela Chair in a baroque interior. It states the chair is "made from many pieces of natural wood, similar to those with which the shacks of the favelas of shanty towns are built in Brazil..." In sum, the Campanas' bilingual press release states that the chair resembles the construction style of Brazilian favelas and infers that such construction is primitive. By describing the chair as a "throne of symbolic elegance," it invites readers to attach whatever additional meaning to the chair they desire.

The Neorustica and Favela Chair press releases include overt references to favelas and uses words like "primitive" or "improvised" to describe the construction aesthetic of these communities. Despite these powerful

20. Press release for the Favela Chair in English and Italian. Provided to the author via email by Julia Tereno, press relations at Estúdio Campana, December 16, 2011.

associations, their texts are brief. The combination of brevity and sweeping generalizations are evidence that the designers believe their readers already possess some distant understanding of what Brazilian favelas are. It is also a sign that this type of favelized marketing does not require specificity or nuance; marketing effectiveness relies on the album of images and meanings about the favela that circulate globally.

In the chapter "Favelization in Fashion," I argued that what the Campanas do (and say) matters. The Campanas have influenced how contemporary Brazilian designers approach and describe their work. Furthermore, referencing Brazil in international marketing pitches is understood today as a viable and successful strategy in luxury marketing in part because of the success of the Campanas. The press release for Neorustica is similar to that pertaining to the Favela Chair in that they both use favelization to market high-end furniture. Like many of the Campanas' projects, Neorustica is supposed to symbolize certain aspects of Brazilian society. The texts in English or Italian address non-Brazilians and ascribe to the designs additional social, cultural, and national meanings.

Elia spent a year working at the Estudio Campana, and there are strong similarities between how Elia describes his work and the vocabulary the Campanas have used to describe theirs. Elia's press kit says the "studio Design Da Gema embodies the pureness of Brazil?s vision, whose epitome is drawn by the vision of its designer." Design da Gema's website states that Elia's designs focus on "reveiling (sic) and giving value to the mundane and everyday aspects of materials, objects appear to reflect the essence of contemporary Brazil that makes trash into luxury." This language is similar to what is often used to describe the Campanas' work. The handout distributed at Friedman Benda (the New York gallery that now represents the brothers) during the opening of the "Concepts" exhibit on June 5, 2013, noted that "the Campana Brothers' work is strongly influenced by their home country, Brazil, and... the Campanas' designs often employ the use of recycled and humble materials, elevating these materials to a higher level in the creation of works that cross cultural boundaries while incorporating themes of transformation and reinvention." These similarities, as well as the similitude between Jahara's description of Neorustica and the Campanas' text for the Favela Chair, perhaps indicate a belief, among younger designers, that this type of vocabulary is effective self-branding. In other words, what worked for the Campanas may work for other Brazilian designers. The Campanas' continued engagement with Brazilian themes may be seen by younger designers as a successful design marketing strategy and one to be emulated.

Elia and Jahara have a strong understanding of the luxury market and the ways in which ideas about contemporary Brazilianness have been used to advertise products to foreign consumers. As a Brazilian designer working in Europe during the early 2000s, Jahara was keenly aware of the Campanas' growing fame. During our interview, he described how his studies and work experiences in Europe coincided with the Campanas' increasing notoriety. Jahara felt that, while he was living outside Brazil, the Campanas were the only Brazilian designers "on the map, showing what is Brazil." The designer admits the Campanas influence his work, particularly their "reuse" of materials and their craft-based practice. However, he says he is "freer of this influence today" and is creating his own visual vocabulary. When asked whether the references to Brazil the Campanas popularized can still be regarded as sources of attached value, Jahara answered that yes, "Brazil is strong." As evidence of the country's popularity, he listed names of several non-Brazilian magazines creating special features on Brazil and cited the country's cultural diversity as one aspect of the Brazilian brand that remains particularly attractive to foreigners. However, Jahara argued that the creation of attached value by referencing Brazil "does not work with the mass market" and is effective only with a "niche [market] that exists in all capitals." In other words, Jahara believes that Brazil as a branding reference is effective only when marketing furniture to the elites of different countries.

It is important to note that favelization is attached to other themes considered in vogue. After spending almost eight years abroad, Jahara said he moved to São Paulo "com vontade de digerir o Brasil" ("with the desire to digest Brazil"). Apart from favelas, the designer talked about the popularity of sustainability. This is an issue Jahara believes Brazilian designers can take the lead on and openly admitted that it was also an effective branding angle. "When you can, say 'sustainable,'"("[q]uando você pode, puxa 'sustainable'") he said. His collection of light fixtures made of used bottle tops and plastic basins is an example of his greater objective: to create limited-edition designs that merge the industrial with the artisanal, and to sell them as luxury objects. Jahara is aware of how references to Brazilian themes (like the favela) and contemporary issues (such as sustainability) are important in the marketing of such products. Elia's use of violence is a similar, albeit more troubling, attempt to create a differentiated application of favelization.

DOMESTICATION

While Torgovnick posited that whites were destined to control and dominate primitive people, in the case of favelization, it is middle- or upper-class Brazilians who are often the ones in a position of power in relation to a darker-skinned and poorer segment of the population. They not only control the socioeconomic conditions of favelas, but also use its reality for its own benefit. Favelization is therefore a commercial form of primitivism; familiar tropes are applied to depictions of favelas to increase the marketability of a product.

Control and domination of the primitive is often manifested through domestication. Favelization sometimes involves the domestication of favelas through objects such as furniture. In *Visualizing American Empire*, Brody studied examples of how the success of Orientalism in the United States "was predicated on Americans bringing fantasies about the cultural Other into their daily lives."[21] With design, domestication often involves the creation and consumption of an object that might signify the primitive but does so in a nonthreatening way. Put simply, domestication allows a consumer to bring home a Favela Chair. The consumer is allowed to own something favela-related that does not involve the perceived dangers of going to a favela or having to interact with favelados. Wealthy consumers are able to bring into their homes objects that reference favelas as evidence of their cosmopolitanism, sophistication, adventurousness, and buying power. Jahara's Neorustica furniture as well as Elia's Pacification and Stray Bullet collections are examples of the domestication of favelas in the form of furniture. They

---

21. Brody, 39.

are also acts of domination over favelas by designers who are light-skinned, educated, middle- or upper-class, and do not live in favelas.

CONCLUSION

The objects discussed in this chapter are examples of how Brazilian designers are reinterpreting definitions of contemporary Brazilianness. These designs, like others that reference favelas and the media that discuss them, are evidence of a deeper cultural shift in which Brazil's poverty and violence are being repositioned as part of its national brand. Favelization might be a sign of inclusion to a certain extent: the poverty that exists in Brazil is being addressed, exposed, or at least mentioned. One could argue that the mere mention of favelas is a sign that these communities are receiving more attention (and not just negative attention). However, there is something else at stake in favelization. The use of references to favelas to brand objects as Brazilian is an act of domination. Torgovnick posits that "[t]he primitive does what we ask it to do. Voiceless, it lets us speak for it. It is our ventriloquist's dummy–or so we like to think."[22] Speaking on behalf of communities that are often voiceless is an act of domination by designers. They superimpose onto favelas the meanings they believe they represent. Words and designs have the power to commodify people, places, and social issues. Torgovnick describes this control over meaning in relation to the primitive: "The real secret of the primitive in this century has often been the same secret as always: the primitive can be–has been, will be (?)–whatever Euro-Americans want it to be. It tells us what we want it to tell us. We decide whether what we

22. Torgovnick, 9.

have heard is a golden confidence or a nasty bit of scandal mongering."[23] The cost of this domination is clear: "[w]hen a people's identity is reduced to caricatures, their real concerns can be more easily dismissed."[24] Unfortunately, design can be a caricature of serious social issues.

It is important to contextualize the trend of favelization in historical and cultural terms. After all, it is not an entirely new phenomenon. In his book *Orientalism*, Edward Said defines orientalism as a colonial way of seeing the world that situates or interprets culture so as to legitimate existing relations of power. Favelization is a process that involves an interpretation of favelas in a manner that legitimates existing relations of power between favelados and residents of formal Brazilian cities. At its worst, favelization is a patronizing and opportunistic way of portraying the reality of favelas. Mostly, when favelas are used, it is not in a manner that would equalize relations of power between those who live in favelas and those who do not.

References to favelas' primitivism and poverty allow marketers to appeal to readers' philanthropic and altruistic motivations. Besides playing on the aesthetic qualities of favelas and the violence within them, the Jahara and Elia press releases describe the objects as having symbolic and narrative functions. They portray the luxury objects as agents of social awareness--symbolic not only of Brazilian culture but also of the socioeconomic difficulties faced by certain individuals in Brazil. Ironically, the profits from the sale of these objects do not, in any manner, benefit the people whose plight

23. Ibid.
24. Floor plan handout, National Museum of the American Indian, New York, NY (2011).

is mentioned in the press releases. However, the press releases' language does lead consumers to believe the purchase of the objects being advertised may somehow benefit favelados.

Favelization is a trend among contemporary Brazilian designers, particularly those who, like Jahara and Elia, understand the international luxury design market. And while Jahara is correct in stating that "design is desire," it is essential to understand how a certain type of longing is manufactured. To use Steele's words, favelization is a situation in which designers mix certain stereotypes about Brazil and favelas "with fantasy and desire in the service of commerce."[25] Favelization is a trend in which these communities and their inhabitants are stereotyped, commodified, and fetishized as an exotic and primitive Other. Complex and subtle problems are inherent in the use of references to favelas by designers who are often white, educated, middle- or upper-class. However, as Sally Price says in *Primitive Art in Civilized Places*, by raising doubts about comfortable assumptions that often surround references to the "exotic" (like favelas) we reveal a cultural-political agenda that is less innocent than it might seem to be.[26] While Brazilian designers and non-Brazilians have the right to derive inspiration from Brazil's landscape, people, history, culture, and socioeconomic realities, consumers and historians of material culture must approach certain trends with a critical eye. As such, favelization requires further evaluation. The origin and end of this trend (if there was or will ever be one) may remain unidentified. However, favelization may entail not only the use of favelas to sell

25. Steele, 119.

26. Sally Price, *Primitive Art in Civilized Places* (Chicago: University of Chicago Press, 2002), 6.

luxury products, but also the commodification of favelas' reality by individuals who dominate the reality of these communities. The use of primitive tropes and stereotypes in Western history during the nineteenth and twentieth centuries begs scholars of material culture, designers, and consumers to pay attention to its potential repetition today.

CONCLUSION

have argued that the process of favelization in design is part of a larger trend in which favelas and favelados are commodified, fetishized, and stereotyped as an exotic and primitive other. I also proposed that favelas have become an oversimplified and exoticized symbol of contemporary Brazilianness. Just as Carmen Miranda was once a stereotypical image, today designers often use references to favelas to brand their projects as Brazilian. The stereotypes of Carnival, sun, beaches, sex, nature, samba, bikini waxes, and soccer have long been associated with Brazil. These stereotypes suggest its culture is flamboyant and permissive. Similarly, casual references to favelas in contemporary culture suggest that these communities are now one of the stereotypes associated with the country. In branding terms, the strategic reference to favelas furthers the image of Brazil as hip, fresh, and daring. A persistent need for the exotic in the marketplace, and the desire to further an image of Brazilian design that stands out in the global design market, have turned a symbol of Brazil's poverty into a signifier of attached value.

A discussion of favelization is bound to be controversial because it challenges myths about Brazilian inter-class cordiality. It requires us to identify who controls the interpretation of favelas, dominates it, and even domesticates it in the form of consumer products. As this book reveals, what one person might regard as an apolitical reference to favelas in a commercial context could be seen as furthering a larger trend that exacerbates the political, economic, and social asymmetry prevalent in Brazil.

In the previous chapters, I discussed the use of references to favelas in film, fashion, and furniture design. I argued that films about favelas provide global audiences with a sense of access to these communities. These films often feature poverty, violence, and crime–familiar tropes of favelization. Despite the growing attention to favelas among academics, film represents the main source of images and stories about these urban spaces for the majority of non–favelados. In my discussion of fashion and furniture, I showed how designers take advantage of the popularity of favelization. The examples I chose reveal an opportunistic portrayal of a certain segment of the Brazilian population by middle- and upper-class Brazilians and non-Brazilians.

Favelization is a trend that requires us to think about the ethics of design. Design is often (maybe even always by) political. Design not only reflects but also *affects* the power relations and human relationships. The projects that employ favelization reflect and affect existing hierarchies of power as well as interactions between individuals of different social status. Some objects are by their very nature political. Others become political because of how they are used, presented, marketed, and branded. The point is not whether a designer intends an object to be political. The fact is that a design becomes political regardless of a designer's original intention. That is most certainly the case with favelization: Each project, artist, designer, and filmmaker has its/his/her own set of objectives, yet favelization is a recognizable trend that requires analysis within a broader context. This is because how we, as designers or consumers, define ourselves and the Other is inseparable from the real, political world.

Designers could ask themselves a series of questions: What kind of attached value am I trying to create? What does a reference to favelas add to my marketing and branding strategy? Have I accurately represented my relationship with the individuals or organization from a favela I am working with? Will this project affect the relative distribution of power, authority, and privilege in a community? The answer might be a simple yes or no. However, it is most likely specific features of the design or marketing that might change the answer to the question (not just the design itself). In other words, a shirt or credenza in and of itself may not affect the power relations between different sectors of Brazilian society. Marketing materials, and especially their reliance on references to favelas, are what may transform the project into a political design that furthers a problematic status quo.

Branding requires the accentuation of differences. It often relies on the processes of dichotomizing, essentializing, and otherizing. This is true of both product branding and national branding. Favelization is a form of both; it applies to products and urban spaces that are treated as a generalizable national stereotype. Yet what is implicit in favelization is the creation of a problematic "us" and "them."

A discussion of favelization forces us to question the representation and the creation of identity. It is an example of how perceived difference is transformed into Otherness, an ever-evolving and multifaceted dynamic that results in actual political, social, and economic consequences for the lives of those identified as Others. Films such as *City of God* and *Waste Land*, the marketing of the Campanas + Lacoste collaboration, the Neorustica furniture line, and Design da Gema's Stray Bullet chair and Pacification shelves are examples of constructions of "the favela" as the Other. They also evidence two additional consequences of otherizing: the commodification of the exotic and the dehumanization of the people identified as Others. By treating all favelas and their inhabitants' realities as interchangeable, favelization strips away their identity. Many design projects that receive international recognition use stories about certain people, instead of the products, to increase the perceived value of goods being sold. An understanding of favelization may help us identify and challenge other design trends that exacerbate stereotypes and unequal power relations. Doing so will further debates about the ethical dimensions of design.

BIBLIOGRAPHY

Abolafio, Beto. "Tempo de Reinventar." *Casa Vogue*, December 2011. Accessed on November 14, 2011. http://www.brunnojahara.com/press.html.

Achebe, Chinua. "An Image of Africa." Paper delivered at a Chancellor's Lecture at the University of Massachusetts, Amherst, on February 18, 1975.

Adams, Beverly. Interview by author, September 14, 2011, New York, NY.

Adelman, Rachel. "'Such Stuff as Dreams Are Made On': God's Footstool in the Aramaic Targumim and Midrashic Tradition." Paper presented at the Annual Meeting for the Society of Biblical Literature, New Orleans, Louisiana, November 21–24, 2009.

Alfred, Darrin, Deyan Sudjic, Li Edelkoort, Stephan Hamel, and Cathy Lang Ho. *Campana Brothers: Complete Works (So Far)*. New York: Rizzoli and Albion Gallery (2010).

Almeida, Marcio Fortes de. *Ministério das Cidades: Plano Nacional de Habitação*. Brasília, Distrito Federal: Secretaria Nacional de Habitação, 2010.

"Alternative Investments in Brazil – The Buys from Brazil: This Year's Hot Market for Private-Equity Firms and Hedge-Fund Managers." *The Economist*, Feb. 15, 2011. http://www.economist.com/node/18178275?story_id=18178275.

Anderson, Benedict. *Imagined Communities: Reflections*

on the Origin and Spread of Nationalism. London: Verso, 1991.

Anderson, Hedvig. "RUM Innovation." *RUM: Tidskriften Om Arkitektur, Inredning & Design*, January 2011. Accessed on November 14, 2011. http://www.brunnojahara.com/press.html.

Angel, Hildegard. "Sucesso do primeiro gala do Brasil em Mônaco garante a segunda edição." *Hildegard Angel*, May 9, 2013. Accessed on August 19, 2013. http://www.hildegardangel.com.br/?p=22131.

"Anticorpos: Fernando & Humberto Campana 1989-2009" exhibit at the Centro Cultural Banco do Brasil, visited by author in São Paulo, Brazil, on January 15, 2012.

Antonelli, Paola, "Projects 66: Campana / Maurer," Museum of Modern Art, 1998. http://www.moma.org/interactives/exhibitions/1998/projects66/.

"A Pedido da Prefeitura, Google faz remoção virtual no mapa do Rio de Janeiro." Website of the Comitê Popular Rio Copa e Olimpíadas, April 7, 2013, http://comitepopulario.wordpress.com/2013/04/07/a-pedido-da-prefeitura-google-faz-remocao-virtual-no-mapa-do-rio-de-janeiro/.

Appadurai, Arjun. *The Social Life of Things: Commodities in Cultural Perspective.* Cambridge: Cambridge University Press, 1997.

"Awards." *Waste Land* website. Accessed on October 15, 2012. http://wastelandmovie.com/awards.html.

"Awards for City of God." IMDB website. Accessed on October 15, 2012. http://www.imdb.com/title/tt0317248.awards.

Azevedo, Aluísio. *The Slum.* Translated by David H. Rosenthal. New York: Oxford University Press, 2000.

Bahia, Silvana. "Palenque BBC: Moradores perdem

casas com teleférico em favela do Rio." *BBC Brasil,* October 10, 2012. http://www.bbc.co.uk/portuguese/noticias/2012/10/121003_palanque_rio_remocoes_bg.shtml.

Bardi, Lina Bo. *Tempos de grossura: O design no impasse.* São Paulo: Instituto Lina Bo e P. M. Bardi, 1994.

Barnes, Taylor. "Rio's shantytowns shrink–on Google Maps, at least." *The Christian Science Monitor.* April 27, 2011. http://www.csmonitor.com/World/Americas/2011/0427/Rio-s-shantytowns-shrink-on-Google-Maps-at-least.

Barringer, Tim and Tom Flynn, eds. *Colonialism and the Object: Empire, Material Culture, and the Museum.* London: Routledge, 1998.

Bauman, Zygmunt. *Wasted Lives: Modernity and Its Outcasts.* Stafford, Australia: Polity Press, 2004.

Bellos, Alex. "And the winner isn't... Katia Lund co-directed the explosive City of God. Why was her name left off the Oscar nomination?" *The Guardian*, February 5, 2004. Accessed on August 23, 2013. http://www.theguardian.com/film/2004/feb/06/oscars.oscars2004.

Bhabha, Homi K. "Cultural Diversity and Cultural Differences." *The Post-Colonial Studies Reader*, ed. Bill Ashcroft, Gareth Griffiths, Helen Tiffin. New York: Routledge, 2006, p. 157.

"Bob Dylan: The Brazil Series." Press release for Statens Museum for Kunst, National Gallery of Denmark, September 4, 2010-January 30, 2011, Copenhagen, Denmark. Obtained by author at Gagosian Gallery, New York.

Booth, Hannah. "Waxing Brazilian." *Design Week* 19 (2004): 14-15.

Borges, Adélia. *Design + Craft: The Brazilian Path*. São Paulo: Editora Terceiro Nome, 2001.

Braga, Marcos da Costa and Ricardo Santos Moreira, eds. *Histórias do Design no Brasil*. São Paulo: Annablume, 2012.

Brasil, Ubiratan, "Catadores recuperam autoestima," *O Estado de São Paulo*, January 21, 2011. http://www.estadao.com.br/noticias/ impresso,catadores-recuperam-autoestima,669029,0.htm.

Brasil, Ubiratan, "Restos se transformam em arte: O documentário Lixo Extraordinário acompanha o trabalho de Vik Muniz com material reciclável," *O Estado de São Paulo*, January 21, 2011. http://www.estadao.com.br/noticias/ impresso,restos-se-transformam-em-arte,669027,0.htm?reload=y.

"Brazil Overview–Context." *The World Bank* (2012). Accessed on October 12, 2012. http://www.worldbank.org/en/country/brazil/ overview.

"Brazilian Photographer Julio Bittencourt to Exhibit at 1500 Gallery September 21, 2011-January 28, 2012." Press release. Obtained by author at 1500 Gallery, 511 West 25th Street, Suite 607, New York, NY 10001.

Brody, David. *Visualizing American Empire: Orientalism and Imperialism in the Philippines*. Chicago: University Of Chicago Press, 2010.

Bruce, Graham. "Alma Brasileira: Music in the Films of Glauber Rocha." In *Brazilian Cinema*, edited by Randal Johnson and Robert Stam, 290-305. Austin: University of Texas, 1988.

Bueno, Laura Machado de Mello. "Contribuição para o conhecimento sobre as favelas no Brasil." Paper presented at the O que é a favela, afinal? conference, Maré, Rio de Janeiro, August 19-20, 2009.

"Buy a Chair Riddled with Brazilian Stray Bullets... On Purpose." *Lost in a Supermarket.* August 12, 2011. Accessed on August 19, 2012. http://lostinasupermarket.com/2011/08/buy-a-chair-riddled-with-stray-bullets-on-purpose/.

Caldeira, Teresa P. R. *City of Walls: Crime, Segregation, and Citizenship in São Paulo.* Berkeley: University of California Press, 2001.

"Campana Brothers." *Arts Review* 10 (2007): 90-93.

Campana, Humberto. *Cartas a um jovem designer: do manual à indústria, a transfusão dos Campana.* Rio de Janeiro: Elsevier (2009).

"Campanas + LACOSTE." *Dezeen.* Accessed on July 2, 2009. http://www.dezeen.com/2009/07/02/campanas-lacoste.

"Campanas + LACOSTE". Lacoste website. Accessed on July 18, 2013. http://www.lacoste.com/campanas/.

Cammilyn.   "Stray   Bullet   chair." *Design Obsession.* August 10, 2011. Accessed on August 19, 2013. http://www.designobsession.net/2011/08/stray-bullet-chair.html.

Cardoso,   Rafael.   Video   clip.   YouTube, http://youtu.be/46rzksttKJ8. Accessed on July 18, 2013. Translated by the author.

Cavallieri, Fernando. "Favelas no Rio: a importância da informação para as políticas públicas." Paper presented at the "O que é a favela, afinal?" conference, Maré, Rio de Janeiro, August 19-20, 2009.

"Chair Design The Stray Bullet Chair." *Trendzona.* Accessed on August 19, 2013. http://trendzona.com/interior-and-furniture/furniture-design/09/chair-design-stray-bullet.html.

Chu, Jeff. "Can a Nightclub Designer Really Make Life Better for the Poor?" *Fast Company.* October 2012. http://www.fastcodesign.com/1670707/marcelo-rosenbaum-may-be-a-little-bit-crazy.

Cipolla, Francisco Paulo. "Luxury Goods Production and Income Concentration: A Discussion of Taylor's Model with Data from Brazil." *Review of Radical Political Economics* 25, no. 3 (1993): 26-33.

Clark, Hazel and David Brody, eds. *Design Studies: A Reader.* New York: Berg, 2009.

"Competition: The Campana Brothers for Lacoste." *Wallpaper* (blog). Accessed on September 15, 2009. http://www.wallpaper.com/fashion/competition-the-campana-brothers-for-lacoste/3686.

"Conquering Complexo do Alemão[:] A Big Step Towards Reclaiming Rio de Janeiro from the Drug Dealers." *The Economist.* December 2, 2010. http://www.economist.com/node/17627963.

Contemporary Art Evening Sale, Auction catalogue. Phillips de Pury & Co., London, June 29, 2008. http://www.phillipsdepury.com/online-catalog.aspx?sn=UK010308.

Coopa-Roca website. Accessed on December 21, 2012, http://www.coopa-roca.org.br.

Correa do Lago, Pedro. *Vik Muniz: Obra completa 1987-2009.* Rio de Janeiro: Capivara Editora Ltda., 2009.

Crepaldi, Iara. "A Decorator for All Seasons." *Tam Nas Nuvens.* May 2012: 74.

Cypriano, Andre. Visit with the artist on November 16, 2012 at Frederico Seve Gallery, 37 West 57th Street, Floor 4, New York, NY 10019.

Daniel, Pete, Merry A. Foresta, Maren Stange, and Sally Stein. *Official Images: New Deal Photography.* Washington, D.C.: Smithsonian Institution Press, 1987.

Davis, Mike. *Planet of Slums*. London: Verso, 2007. Kindle edition.

"Dedo Verde: Batucada." *Joyce Pascovitch*, September 2011. Accessed on November 14, 2011. http://www.brunnojahara.com/press.html.

Derringer, Jaime. "Stray Bullet Chair by Design da Gema." *Design Milk*, August 9, 2011. Accessed on August 19, 2013. http://design-milk.com/stray-bullet-chair-by-design-da-gema.

"Design Brazil" exhibit, flyer. Design Flanders Gallery, Brussels, Belgium, November 12, 2011-February 5, 2012. The exhibition was part of the program *Europalia. Brasil*. Given to author by the curator, Tulio Mariante, in Rio de Janeiro, Brazil.

Design da Gema website. Accessed on August 23, 2013. www.designdagema.com.

"Design da Gema." *ICON Magazine*. November 2011, Issue 101. Accessed on Design da Gema's website on August 23, 2013. http://www.designdagema.com/#clipping.

"Development of Rio de Janeiro." *Unlocking Archives: Royal Geographical Society with The Institute of British Geographers*. Accessed on October 12, 2012. http://www.unlockingthearchives.rgs.org/themes/brazil/factsheets/resource/?id=573.

"Design–Editor's Pick: Neorustica by Brunno Jahara." *Because London*, November 24, 2010. Accessed on November 14, 2011. http://www.brunnojahara.com/press.html.

Dilnot, Clive. "The Critical in Design (Part One)." *Journal of Writing in Creative Practice* 1, no. 2 (2008): 177-89.

Duarte, Cristovão. "A "reinvenção" da cidade a partir dos espaços populares." Paper presented at the "*O que é a favela, afinal?* conference, Maré, Rio de Janeiro, August 19-20, 2009.

Duarte, Frederico. "Beyond the Fruit Hat: Brazilian Product and Furniture Design Today." Presentation delivered at the School of Visual Art's MFA Design Criticism symposium Crossing the Line: The 2010 D-Crit Conference (April 30th, 2010), http://www.alvorada.org/2010/05/alvorada-in-9-minutes/.

Duarte, Frederico. "Fator Favela." *Projeto Design* 376 (June 2011).

Edwards, Meghan. "The Way Forward 2010." *Interior Design* 81.15 (2010): 158-95.

"Eike Batista, The Salesman of Brazil: A Big Step towards Reclaiming Rio de Janeiro from the Drug Dealers." *The Economist.* May 26, 2012. http://www.economist.com/node/215555907.

Elia, David. "RE: Follow-up questions." Message to the author. August 17, 2013. E-mail.

——. "RE: Info." Message to the author. August 15, 2013. E-mail.

——. "RE: Luxury Conference". Message to the author. March 11, 2012. E-mail.

——. "RE: Mark Magaril (LinkedIn)." Message to the author. February 1 and 20, 2011; May 12 and 13, 2011; December 5, 2011; . E-mail.

——. "RE: Pergunta". Message to the author. March 14, 2012. E-mail.

Enwezor, Okuwi. "The Postcolonial Constellation: Contemporary Art in a State of Permanent Transition." *Research in African Literatures* 34, no. 4 (Winter 2003): 57-82.

Errington, Shelly. *The Death of Authentic Primitive Art:*

And Other Tales of Progress. Berkeley: University of California Press, 1998.

"Fernando e Humberto Campana: Favela, Edra." *Abitare* 429 (2003): 163.

Frank, Robert H. *Luxury Fever: Weighing the Cost of Excess.* Princeton, NJ: Princeton University Press, 2000.

"Fratelli Campana." *Abitare* 351 (1996): 202-4.

"Fresh[:] Three Playful Ideas." *Functional Fate,* May 2011. Blog post not found online, but a passive image was available on Design da Gema's website. http://www.designdagema.com/#clipping.

Furtado, Celso. *The Economic Growth of Brazil: A Survey from Colonial to Modern Times.* Los Angeles: University of California Press, 1968.

Gatti, Andre. "City of God: A Landmark in Brazilian Film Language." *City of God in Several Voices: Brazilian Social Cinema as Action.* Edited by Else R.P. Viera. Hong Kong: BookCyclone, 2011. Kindle Edition.

Gilligan, Melanie. "Slumsploitation: The Favela on Film and TV." *Mute* 2, no. 3, 2006, http://www.metamute.org/editorial/articles/slumsploitation-favela-film-and-tv.

Goñi, Edwin, J. Humberto Lopez, and Luis Servén. "Fiscal Redistribution and Income Inequality in Latin America." *The World Bank* (2008): 19-30.

Gonzalez, Laura. "RE: Important question." Message to the author. August 12, 2013. Email.

Grant. "Neorustica Furniture," *D-Build: Deconstruct, Design, Develop,* December 8, 2010. Accessed on November 14, 2011. http://www.brunnojahara.com/press.html.

Hall, Stuart. *Representation: Cultural Representations and Signifying Practices.* Thousand Oaks, CA: Sage Publications & Open University, 1997.

Ho, Cathy Lang. "Brothers of Invention." *The International Design Magazine* 50 (2003), http://search.proquest.com/docview/66410367?accountid=12261.

Ho, Cathy Lang. "The Boys from Brazil," *ArtBistro*, October 12, 2009, http://artbistro.monster.com/news/articles/9309-the-boys-from-brazil?page=1.

Holden, Stephen. "From a Universe of Trash, Recycling Art and Hope," *The New York Times*, October 28, 2010, http://movies.nytimes.com/2010/10/29/movies/29waste.html?ref=movies.

Hollanda, Heloisa Buarque de. "Entrevista com Paulo Lins." *Heloisa Buarque de Hollanda.* September 15, year not stated. Accessed on August 23, 2013. http://www.heloisabuarquedehollanda.com.br/entrevista-a-paulo-lins.

Holston, James, ed. *Cities and Citizenship (A Public Culture Book).* Durham, NC: Duke University Press Books, 1998.

Holston, James. *Insurgent Citizenship: Disjunctions of Democracy and Modernity in Brazil.* Princeton, NJ: Princeton University Press, 2007.

Ho, Matt. "Stray Bullet Chair Takes After a Shoot 'em Up Design." *Trendhunter.* August 10, 2011. Accessed on August 19, 2013. http://www.trendhunter.com/trends/stray-bullet-chair.

hooks, bell. *Where We Stand: Class Matters.* London: Routledge, 2000.

Hui, Ban. "Neorustica Furniture Collection." *Casa International: Architecture Interiors Design Arts*, January 2, 2011. Accessed on November 14, 2011, http://www.brunnojahara.com/press.html.

"Income Inequality." *The Economist*, April 20, 2011,

http://www.economist.com/node/
18587127?story_id=18587127&CFID=163009207&CFTOKEN=11815028.

"In-store –The Campana Brothers for Lacoste." *The New York Times* (blog), Nov. 4 2009. http://tmagazine.blogs.nytimes.com/2009/11/04/in-store-the-campana-brothers-for-lacoste/.

Jahara, Brunno. Interview by author. Handwritten notes. São Paulo, Brazil, January 5, 2012.

Jahara Studio website, Accessed on November 14, 2011, http://www.brunnojahara.com.

"Jahara Studio: Meblez Brazylijskich Favela." Etnodizajn Festiwal website, November 29, 2010. Accessed on November 14, 2011. http://www.brunnojahara.com/press.html.

"Jahara Studio: Neorustica Furniture Collection." *Designboom*, November 23, 2010. Accessed on November 14, 2011. http://www.brunnojahara.com/press.html.

"Jahara Studio." *The Sin Freno Company*, November 29, 2010. Accessed on November 14, 2011. http://www.brunnojahara.com/press.html.

Johnson, Randal and Robert Stam, eds. *Brazilian Cinema*. Austin: University of Texas Press, 1988.

Karp, Ivan and Steven Levine, eds. *Exhibiting Cultures: The Poetics and Politics of Museum Display*. Washington, DC: Smithsonian Books, 1991.

Kirshenblatt-Gimblett, Barbara. *Destination Culture: Tourism, Museums, and Heritage*. Berkeley: University of California Press, 1998.

Khemsurov, Monica. "The World's Top Emerging Furniture-Makers: A Collector's Guide to the 10 Firms You Need to Know." *Details*, April 2011. Accessed on November 14, 2011. http://www.brunnojahara.com/press.html.

Lago, Pedro Corrêa do. *Vik Muniz: Obra Competa 1987-2009,* Rio de Janeiro: Capivara Editora Ltda., 2009.

Lara, Fernando Luiz. "Modernism Made Vernacular: The Brazilian Case." *Journal of Architectural Education* 63.1 (2009): 41-50.

"Vila Viva Favela Redesign." Lecture at Parsons the New School For Design, November 2, 2011, New York, NY.

Latin America. Auction catalogue. New York: Phillips de Pury & Company, November 2011. Lavigne, Nathalia. "Natureza Transformada." *Tam Nas Nuvens.* May 2012: 88.

Leal, Maria Teresa. Interview by author. Handwritten notes. Rio de Janeiro, Brazil, January 3, 2012.

Leitão, Gerônimo. "Quem conhece uma favela, conhece todas?" Paper presented at the "O que é a favela, afinal?" conference, Maré, Rio de Janeiro, August 19-20, 2009.

Leopoldo. Tour by Favela Tours. Rio de Janeiro, Brazil, December 30, 2011.

Lesser, Jeffrey. *Negotiating National Identity: Immigrants, Minorities, and the Struggle for Ethnicity in Brazil.* Durham, NC: Duke University Press, 1999.

Levy, Michele. "Taxis & Mystery Recycling Boxes." Message to the author. October 19, 2011. Email.

Lima, Guilherme Cunha. "Pioneers of Brazilian design." Paper presented at the 8th Conference of the International Committee for Design History and Design Studies, São Paulo, Brazil, September 4-6, 2012.

"Lucy Walker, Director." *Waste Land* website. Accessed on July 18, 2013. http://wastelandmovie.com/lucy-walker.html.

Mariante, Tulio. Interview by author. Handwritten notes. Rio de Janeiro, Brazil, December 29, 2011.

Matter, Martin. "Brazil's Economy: An Introduction." *Swiss Business HUB Brazil* (2012): 1-5. Accessed on October 12, 2012. http://www.osec.ch/de/filefield-private/files/553/field_blog_public_files/12398.

Maurício, Ivan. "Enciclopédia Nordeste: Favela Urbana." *O Nordeste*. Accessed on October 12, 2012. http://www.onordeste.com/onordeste/ enciclopediaNordeste/index.php?titulo=Favela.

McKinlay, Sophie. "Out of the Ordinary." *Modern Carpets + Textiles* (2007): 32-7.

Meirelles, Fernando. "Writing the Script, Finding and Preparing the Actors." *City of God in Several Voices: Brazilian Social Cinema as Action*. Edited by Else R.P. Viera. Hong Kong: BookCyclone, 2011. Kindle Edition.

Melo, Nicole Maria Turcheti E. "Public Policy for the Favelas in Rio de Janeiro: The Problem (in) Framing." M.A. diss., International Institute of Social Studies, 2010. Accessed on October 12, 2012. http://hdl.handle.net/ 2105/8698.

Minh-ha, Trinh T. *When the Moon Waxes Red: Representation, Gender, and Cultural Politics*. New York: Routledge, 1991.

Molinari, Fernando, dir. "Coopa-Roca e Lacroix: Exposição Um Salão Francês–Roda da Moda." Video of the exhibit *Salão Francês: uma colaboração XCLC e COOPA-ROCA*. Accessed on August 23, 2013. http://www.youtube.com/watch?v=uXRor4iuyt4.

"Mundo Verde." *RG*, October 2010. Accessed on November 14, 2011. http://www.brunnojahara.com/ press.html.

Muniz, Vik. "Campana Brothers," *Bomb* 102 (Winter 2008), http://bombsite.com/issues/102/articles/3040.

——. *Lixo Extraordinário*. Rio de Janeiro: G. Ermakoff Casa Editorial, 2010.

Musetto, V.A. "Waste Land," *New York Post*, October 28, 2010 and updated October 31, 2010, http://www.nypost.com/p/entertainment/movies/waste_land_zlyh9vSpmkNADzhSsRr1VN#ixzz1uD8nnEpS.

Nagib, Lucia. "Talking Bullets: The Language of Violence in City of God." *City of God in Several Voices: Brazilian Social Cinema as Action.* Edited by Else R.P. Viera. Hong Kong: BookCyclone, 2011. Kindle Edition.

Nakajima, Kyoko. "The Palette of the Amazon." *Axis* 111 (2004): 72-6.

National Museum of the American Indian, Museum plan. Smithsonian Institution, New York, New York. George Gustav Heye Center. Picked up by author during visit in 2012."Neorustica by Jahara Studio." *Dezeen Design Magazine*, November 25, 2010. Accessed on November 14, 2011. http://www.brunnojahara.com/press.html.

"Neorustica by Jahara Studio." *Furnishh!*, November 25, 2010. Accessed on November 14, 2011, http://www.brunnojahara.com/press.html.

"Neorustica Furniture Collection International Premiere." *DeTnk*, November 29, 2010. Accessed on November 14, 2011. http://www.brunnojahara.com/press.html.

"Neorustica Furniture." *SHFT: Curating the Culture of Today's Environment*, December 5, 2010. Accessed on November 14, 2011. http://www.brunnojahara.com/press.html.

Nós do Cinema's website. Accessed on August 23, 2013, http://www.dreamscanbe.org/view/338.

Ogbechie, Sylvester Okwunodu. "Ordering the Universe: Documenta 11 and the Apotheosis of the Occidental Gaze." *Art Journal* 64, no. 1 (Spring 2005): 80-89.

O'Hehir, Andrew. "Who Really Made the Oscar-Nominated "Waste Land"? Unpacking the rumors around Lucy Walker's acclaimed garbage documentary," *Salon*, February 24, 2011, http://www.salon.com/2011/02/24/waste_land.

Okonkwo, Uche. *Luxury Fashion Branding: Trends, Tactics, Techniques*. New York: Palgrave Macmillan, 2007.

"ONU acusa Brasil de desalojar pessoas à força por conta da Copa e Olimpíada." *Estadão.com.br*, April 26, 2011. http://www.estadao.com.br/noticias/esportes,onu-acusa-brasil-de-desalojar-pessoas-a-forca-por-conta-da-copa-e-olimpiada,710895,0.htm.

Oppenheimer, Jean. "Shooting the Real: Boys from Brazil." *City of God in Several Voices: Brazilian Social Cinema*. Edited by Else Viera. Hong Kong: BookCyclone, 2011. Kindle Edition.

"O que é a favela, afinal? by Observatório de Favelas." Introduction presented at the "O que é a favela, afinal?" conference, Maré, Rio de Janeiro, August 19-20, 2009.

Oricchio, Luiz Zanin. "Um filme, três autores: João Jardim fala da rotina de filmagem do documentário Lixo Extraordinário," *O Estado de São Paulo*, January 26, 2011, http://www.estadao.com.br/noticias/impresso,um-filmetres-autores,671106,0.htm.

Osovskava, Julia. "Stray Bullet Chair by Design da Gema." *Chair Blog*. August 23, 2011. Accessed on August 19, 2013, http://www.chairblog.eu/2011/08/stray-bullet-chair-by-design-da-gema.

Park, Lisa Sun-Hee and David Pellow. *Slums of Aspen: Immigrants vs. the Environment in America's Eden*. New York: New York University Press, 2011. Kindle edition.

Paul, Donna. "Favela Forever." *Interior Design* 76.1 (2005): 263.

Paul, Rebecca. "Brunno Jahara Turns Salvaged Wood

into Vibrant Furniture Full of Character." *Inhabitat*, December 23, 2010. Accessed on November 14, 2011, http://www.brunnojahara.com/press.html.

Pedrosa, Adriano, ed. *ArtNexusBrasil en Colombia.* Bogotá, Colombia: Arte en Colombia SAS, 2011.

Penna-Firme, Rodrigo and Eduardo Brondizio. "The Risks of Commodifying Poverty: Rural Communities, *Quilombola* Identity, and Nature Conservation in Brazil." *Habitus* 5, no. 2 (July/December 2007): 355-73.

Perlman, Janice. *Favela: Four Decades of Living on the Edge in Rio de Janeiro.* New York: Oxford University Press, 2011. Kindle edition.

"Planeta Casa: Ideas e produtos para um mundo sustentável." *Casa Claudia,* April 2011. Accessed on November 14, 2011, http://www.brunnojahara.com/press.html.

Price, Sally. *Primitive Art in Civilized Places.* Chicago: Chicago University Press, 2002.

"Production Company." *Waste Land* website. July 18, 2013.   http://wastelandmovie.com/production-company.html.

Projeto Morrinho. Video screening and panel discussion, Brazilian Endowment for the Arts, New York, NY, September 20, 2012.

Rangel, Gabriela, ed. *Dias & Riedweg... And It Becomes Something Else.* New York: Americas Society, 2010.

Raskin, Jonah. *The Mythology of Imperialism.* New York: Random House, 1971.

Revista abcDesign, January 5, 2011. Accessed on November 14, 2011, http://www.brunnojahara.com/press.html.

Rezende, Livia. "Crafting the Nation: Brazilian 'Civilised Exoticism' at World Exhibitions." *Design and Craft: A History of Convergences and Divergence.* Edited by

Javier Gimeno-Martinez and Fredie Floré. Brussels: Universa, 2010.

"Rio de Janeiro[:] Hoping for the Best; Preparing for the Worst." *The Economist.* January 3, 2011. http://www.economist.com/blogs/americasview/2011/01/rio_de_janeiro.

Roberts, Michael. *Carlos Miele.* Published in connection with the 2008 spring and summer collections by Carlos Miele Studio.

Rocha, Glauber. "An Esthetic of Hunger." *Brazilian Cinema.* Edited by Randal Johnson and Robert Stam. Austin: University of Texas, 1988.

Romanelli, Marco, and M. Estrada. 1991. "Il disegno del mobile brasiliano: Appunti di viaggio." *Domus*, No. 728, June 1991: 70-XXII.

Romero, Simon. "In Brazil, Streets of Dancing Cars and Swagger." *The New York Times.* March 30, 2013, http://www.nytimes.com/2013/03/31/world/americas/lowrider-culture-spreads-to-brazil-and-beyond.html?_r=0.

Roux, Caroline. "Interview: Campana Brothers." *Blueprint* 257: 2007, 54-57, http://search.proquest.com/docview/66498744?accountid=12261.

Rude, Kelly. "Discovering Brazil." *Canadian Interiors* 41, 2004: 30-35, http://search.proquest.com/docview/66344951?accountid=12261.

Rudofsky, Bernard. *Architecture Without Architects.* New York: Museum of Modern Art, 1964.

Said, Edward W. *Orientalism.* New York: Vintage, 1979.

——. *Power, Politics and Culture.* New York: Vintage, 2002. Kindle Edition.

——. *Representations of the Intellectual: The 1992 Reith Lectures.* New York: Vintage, 1996.

Schonberger, Nick. "Stray Bullet Chair." *Complex*. August 22, 2011. Accessed on August 19, 2013. http://www.complex.com/art-design/2011/08/stray-bullet-chair.

Schroeter, Sara, producer. "The World of Carlos Miele." Video. New York: Vogue TV, 2010. DVD copy obtained by author through Ben Rousseaua, public relations representative of the Carlos Miele New York store.

Scorch. "Design da Gema–Stray Bullet Chair." *Movements and Nonsense*. August 10, 2011. Accessed on August 23, 2013. http://movementsandnonsense.com/2011/08/design-da-gema-stray-bullet-chair/.

Sekula, Allan. *Dismal Science: Photo Works, 1972 - 1996*. Normal, IL: University Galleries of Illinois State University, 1999.

Sekula, Allan. *Photography Against the Grain: Essays and Photo Works 1973-1983*. Halifax: Press of the Novia Scotia College of Art and Design, 1984.

"Sem UPP, algum resquácio de tráfico permanece no Alemão, diz ONG." *Radio Estadão ESPN*. Accessed on October 15, 2012, http://radio.estadao.com.br/audio.php?idGuidSelect=9D031C45802D4C2497A57F3C28C79B39.

Seo, Jae Woo. "Jahara Studio in Brazil." *J.J. Magazine*, April 2011. Accessed on November 14, 2011, http://www.brunnojahara.com/press.html.

Shahad. "Stray Bullet Chair // Design da Gema." *Visual Therapy*, August 2011. Accessed on August 19, 2013, http://www.visualtherapyonline.com/?p=17791.

Silva, Camila Assis Peres and Guilherme Cunha Lima. "From the Improvisation to the Solution: The Design in the Casual Market of the City of Rio de Janeiro." Paper presented at the 8th Conference of the International

Committee for Design History and Design Studies, São Paulo, Brazil, September 4-6, 2012.

Silva, Renato Josivaldo da. Tour by Favela Adventures. Rio de Janeiro, Brazil, January 2, 2012.

Smith, Cynthia.*Design with the Other 90% Cities*. New York: Smithsonian Institution, Cooper-Hewitt, National Design Museum, 2011.

"Some Clever Ideas." *Creative Review* 27.4 (2007): 32-3.

Staff, Joia. "Stray Bullet, la silla tiro al blanco." *Joia Magazine*, August 9, 2011. Accessed on August 19, 2013, http://www.joiamagazine.com/tag/stray-bullet.

Stam, Robert. *Tropical Multiculturalism: A Comparative History of Race in Brazilian Cinema & Culture*, Durham, NC: Duke University Press, 1997.

"Stray Bullet Chair by Design da Gema Survived a Fake Shot." *Furnime*. Accessed on August 19, 2013, http://www.furnime.com/stray-bullet-chair-by-design-da-gema-survived-a-fake-shot-005133.html.

Tagg, John. *The Burden of Representation: Essays on Photographies and Histories*. Amherst: University of Massachusetts Press, 1988.

TanYa."The Stray Bullet Chair by Design da Gema." *Bedzine*. August 12, 2011. Accessed on August 23, 2013, http://bedzine.com/blog/bed-furniture/chairs/the-stray-bullet-chair-by-design-da-gema/.

Torgovnick, Mariana. *Gone Primitive: Savage Intellects, Modern Lives*. Chicago: University of Chicago Press, 1991.

Tommasini, Maria and Francesca Picchi. "Design Morbido./Soft Design." *Domus* 848 (2002), May 2002.

Urry, John. "Gazing on History." *The Tourist Gaze; Leisure and Travel in Contemporary Societies*. London: Sage, 1990.

Valladares, Licia do Prado. Introduction to *A invenção*

da favela: do mito de origem à favela. Rio de Janeiro: Editora FGV, 2005.

Vellest, Ray. "Bala Perdida Chair by Design da Gema." *Woordup.* Accessed on August 23, 2013, http://woordup.com/2011/01/08/bala-perdida-chair-by-design-da-gema.

Ventura, Zuenir. *Cidade Partida.* São Paulo: Companhia das Letras, 1994.

Viera, Else, ed., *City of God in Several Voices: Brazilian Social Cinema as Action.* Hong Kong: BookCyclone, 2011. Kindle Edition.

Viladas, Pilar. "Now Showing–Design Fever." *New York Times* (blog), May 13, 2011. Accessed on November 14, 2011, http://www.brunnojahara.com/press.html.

Voight, Rebecca. "The Campana Brothers Save Lacoste's Skin." *Interview Magazine* (blog), June 7, 2009, http://www.interviewmagazine.com/blogs/fashion/2009-07-06/campana-lacoste/.

Walker, John. "Defining the Object of Study." *Design Reader.* Oxford: Berg Publishers, 2009.

"'Waste Land,' Documentary on Brooklyn Artist and Rio's Garbage Pickers," *Huffington Post,* first posted May 25, 2010 and updated November 17, 2010, http://www.huffingtonpost.com/2010/11/17/waste-land-documentary-on_n_785175.html.

"Wastemaker," *Wallpaper,* April 2011: 56.

Williams, Lyneise E. "Heavy Metal: Decoding Hip Hop Jewelry." *Metalsmith* 27, no. 1 (2007).

Winner, Langdon. *The Whale and the Reactor: A Search for Limits in an Age of High Technology.* Chicago: University of Chicago Press, 1986. http://zaphod.mindlab.umd.edu/docSeminar/pdfs/Winner.pdf

Zeiderman, Austin. "The Fetish and the Favela: Notes on Tourism and the Commodification of Place in Rio de

Janeiro, Brazil." Paper presented at the 2006 Breslauer Graduate Student Symposium, The Right to the City and the Politics of Space, sponsored by the University of California International and Area Studies, Berkeley, California, April 14-15, 2006. http://escholarship.org/uc/item/11q523gj.

Zygmunt, Bauman. *Wasted Lives: Modernity and Its Outcasts.* Stafford, Australia: Polity Press, 2004.

"2010 Census improved identification of subnormal agglomerates." IBGE, July 18, 2013, http://ibge.gov.br/english/presidencia/noticias/noticia_visualiza.php?id_noticia=2051&id+pagina=1.

"2011 Global Study on Homicide." ONODC, Accessed on October 15, 2012, http://www.unodcorg/southerncone/en/frontpage/2011/10/06-global-study-on-homicide-2011.html.

ACKNOWLEDGMENTS

I would like to thank the Cooper Hewitt, National Design Museum (Smithsonian Institution) for publishing the first edition of this book as part of the DesignFile series on February 11, 2014.

Thank you to Penny Wolfson, my editor, and David Brody, Sarah Lichtman, Laura Auricchio, Clive Dilnot, Freya Hartzell, and Marilyn Cohen for helping me workshop different parts of this book. Your comments were essential in helping me strengthen my arguments and improve the text. Thank you to Jilli Traganou, Lowery Stokes Sims, Natalie Balthrop, Sarah Mallory, Augusto Lima, Mark Sze, Jeffrey Head, and Meg Weeks for your comments and to Jayun Cho for creating www.favelization.net. Rachel Cassiman, this project would not have been possible without your research assistance. I am grateful for the many friends and family that supported me during the entire publishing process. This book is dedicated to Barry "Ricardo" Goldman who helps me believe in myself, for enduring the stress involved with this project, and joining me on this journey.

A special *obrigada* to all producers of contemporary Brazilian culture, in Brazil and abroad. It is your creativity, courage, and determination that allows academics like myself to do our work.

ABOUT THE AUTHOR

Adriana has a B.A. from Brown University, a J.D. from Georgetown University Law Center, and an M.A. in the History of Decorative Arts and Design from Parsons The New School for Design and Cooper-Hewitt, National Design Museum. She is originally from São Paulo and now lives in New York with her husband and their dog, Cachaça. www.adrianakertzer.com

SOCIAL MEDIA

Follow the on-going conversation on-line:
    Website: favelization.net
    Twitter: @favelization
    Pinterest: pinterest.com/adrianakertzer/favelization/
    Facebook: facebook.com/favelization